## FESTIVALS / EVENTS

**January**
Transmediale
*www.transmediale.de*
Berlin Fashion Week (also in July)
*www.fashion-week-berlin.com*
CTM Festival
*www.ctm-festival.de*

**February**
Berlin International Film Festival
*www.berlinale.de*

**March**
Long Night of the Museums
*www.lange-nacht-der-museen.de*
Fantasy Filmfest
*www.fantasyfilmfest.com*
MaerzMusik
*www.berlinerfestspiele.de*

**April**
Pictoplasma Berlin (through to May)
*berlin.pictoplasma.com*

**May/June**
DMY International Design Festival
*www.dmy-berlin.com*
48 Hours Neukölln
*www.48-stunden-neukoelln.de*

**August**
International Berlin Beer Festival
*www.bierfestival-berlin.de*

**September**
Berlin Music Week
*www.berlin-music-week.de*
Berlin Art Week
*www.berlinartweek.de*
abc Art Berlin Contemporary (#18)
*www.artberlincontemporary.com*

**Irregular dates**
Berlin Biennale
*www.berlinbiennale.de*

Event days vary by year. Please check for updates online.

## UNUSUAL OUTINGS

Alternative Berlin Tours
*alternativeberlin.com*

Bauhaus Excursions
*www.artberlin-online.de*

Berlin Underworld (#11)
*berliner-unterwelten.de*

Creative Sustainability Tours
*creative-sustainability-tours-berlin.net*

Finding Berlin Tours
*www.findingberlin-tours.com*

The Hidden Path
*thehiddenpath.de*

Niche Art & Architecture Tours Berlin
*nicheberlin.de*

## SMARTPHONE APP

**Street art tracker**
Street art berlin

**Train map & route planner**
Berlin Subway

**Biking journal & navigator**
bbybike

## REGULAR EXPENSES

**Adult single ticket (zone AB, 2-hr train/bus)**
€2.60

**Domestic letters / EU & International airmail**
€0.60/0.75

**Gratuities**
Diners: optional 5-10% in cash as you pay
Hotels: €1-2 for the porter, €1-2 for cleaners
Licensed taxis: 10%

# Count to 10

## What makes Berlin so special?
Illustrations by Guillaume Kashima aka Funny Fun

See what Berlin creatives consider essential to see, taste, read and take home from your trip, whether you are on a one-day stopover or a week-long stay. The graffiti-wrapped cultural capital always has something for every taste. Bread, books, history, museums, architecture and underground clubs – just put on your best shoes and enjoy.

## 1

### Architecture

**Stiftung Denkmal für die ermordeten Juden Europas**
*by Peter Eisenman*

**Reichstag**
*by Norman Foster*

**DZ Bank Berlin (Pariser pl. 3)**
*by Gehry Partners*

**Exhibition hall (extension) at Deutsches Historisches Museum (#4)**
*by I. M. Pei.*

**Neue Nationalgalerie**
*by Ludwig Mies van der Rohe*

**Berliner Fernsehturm**
*by Hermann Henselmann*

Berlin is swiftly becoming an epicentre for creative culture, pulsing with ideas and inspiration. The city's complicated history is one underlying force that propels the city, while a natural sense for precision and rationality is another. People of the city are keen to live in the moment, learn and make a better life, as international artists fly in regularly to soak up the energy, and become part of the radical change.

**CITIx60: Berlin** explores the German capital in five aspects, covering architecture, art spaces, shops and markets, eating and entertainments. With expert advice from 60 stars of Berlin's creative scene, this book guides you to the real attractions of the city for an authentic taste of Berlin life.

**Contents**

**002** **Before You Go**
Basic information, festivals and useful apps

**004** **Count to 10**
What makes Berlin so special?

**009** **60X60**
60 Local Creatives X 60 Hotspots
- Landmarks & Architecture
- Cultural & Art Space
- Markets & Shops
- Restaurants & Cafés
- Nightlife

**102** **District Maps**
60 hotspots at a glance

**112** **Accommodations**
Hip hostels, fully-equipped apartments & swanky hotels

**116** **Notepad**
Blank paper for sketches and remarks

# Before You Go

## BASIC INFO

**Currency**
Euro (EUR/€)
Exchange rate: €1 : $1.4

**Time zone**
GMT +1
DST +2

DST begins at 0200 (local time) on the last Sunday of March and ends at 0300 (local time) on the last Sunday of October.

**Dialling**
International calling: +49
Citywide: (0)30

*Dial (0) for calls made within Germany.

**Weather (avg. temperature range)**
Spring (Mar-May): 3-13°C / 37-55°F
Summer (Jun-Aug): 14-25°C / 57-77°F
Autumn (Sep-Nov): 5-15°C / 41-59°F
Winter (Dec-Feb): -3-2°C / 27-36°F

## USEFUL WEBSITES

**Interactive Railway Route Map (DE)**
www.fahrinfo-berlin.de/Liniennetz

**Prepaid SIM card**
blau.de

## EMERGENCY CALLS

**Ambulance & fire**
112

**Police**
110

**Embassies & Consulates**
China     +49 (0)30 27 58 80
Japan     +49 (0)30 21 09 40
France    +49 (0)30 59 00 39 000
UK        +49 (0)30 20 45 70
US        +49 (0)30 83 050

## AIRPORT EXPRESS TRANSFER

**Tegal <-> Alexanderplatz (JetExpressBus TXL)**
Bus / Journey: every 10-20 mins / 45 mins
From Tegel Airport – 0438-0028
From Alexanderplatz – 0452-2307 (Sa-Su: 0552-)
One-way: €2.60/1.60

**Schönefeld <-> Alexanderplatz (RB14)**
Train / Journey: hourly / 30 mins
From Schönefeld Airport – 0403-2026 (M-F), -1526 (Sa), -1926 (Su)
From Alexanderplatz – 0413-2013 (M-F), -1614 (Sa), -1913 (Su)
One-way (Berlin ABC): €3.20/2.30

*www.berlin-airport.de, www.vbb.de*
New Berlin Brandenburg Airport is scheduled to open in 2015.

## PUBLIC TRANSPORT IN BERLIN

Railways (U-Bahn/S-Bahn)
Tram
Bus
Bike
Taxi

**Means of Payment**
Credit cards (ticketing)
Cash

Tickets must be validated before use. Day tickets are valid until 0300 the next morning.

## PUBLIC HOLIDAYS

| | |
|---|---|
| January | 1 New Year's Day |
| March/April | Good Friday, Easter Monday |
| May | 1 Labour Day, Ascension Day |
| May/June | Whit Monday |
| October | 3 German Unity Day |
| December | 25 Christmas Day, 26 Boxing Day |

Museums and galleries might have varied opening hours on public holidays.

## 2
### Historical Landmarks

**Jüdisches Museum Berlin**
www.jmberlin.de

**East Side Gallery & Berliner Mauer**
www.eastsidegallery-berlin.de

**Gedenkstätte und Museum Sachsenhausen**
www.stiftung-bg.de/gums/index.htm

**DDR Museum**
www.ddr-museum.de

**Topographie des Terrors**
www.topographie.de

**Sowjetisches Ehrenmal (#1)**
Treptower Park,
Alt-Treptow, 12435

## 3
### Street Art Hunting

**Plattenbauten by Evol**
www.evoltaste.com

**Blu**
blublu.org

**ROA**
www.flickr.com/people/roagraffiti

**Vhils**
www.alexandrefarto.com

**NELIO**
neli0.tumblr.com

**Awer**
awerart.tumblr.com

**SuperBlast**
www.superblast.de

**Mentalgassi**
mentalgassi.blogspot.hk

## 4
### Market

**Markthalle Neun (#36)**
Street food & drink
Rhabarberschorle (Fizzy Rhubarb)

**Trödelmarkt Arkonaplatz (#34)**
Vintage home accessories &
German postcards

**Mauerpark Flohmarkt**
Classic treasures
www.mauerparkmarkt.de

**Boxhagener Platz Wochen Markt**
Good choice of fresh food
www.boxhagenerplatz.de

**Antik und Buchmarkt am Bode-Museum (#14)**
Antiques & Books
www.antik-buchmarkt.de

## Book & Record Store

**Artist publications**
Motto Berlin (#29)

**Handmade comics**
Neurotitan
www.neurotitan.de

**Reading room & bookshop**
do you read me?
www.doyoureadme.de

**Design, art & architechture**
Pro QM
www.pro-qm.de

**Design books & workshops**
Gestalten Space
news.gestalten.com/space

**Rare records & vinyls**
Hard Wax
hardwax.com

## Nourishment

**Bockwurst & smoked fish**
Treptower Park's pier

**Currywurst with Schrippe (bread roll)**
Neurotitan
www.konnopke-imbiss.de

**Milk Broiled Chicken**
Henne
www.henne-berlin.de

**Homemade Gözleme & Lahmacun**
Imren Grill
Karl-Marxstr. 80, Neukölln, 12043

**Döner Kebab**
Mustafa
www.mustafas.de

**Club Mate (Winter edition)**
Any späti around Christmas

## Bread

**Sourdough bread**
Bread Exchange (barter only!)
thebreadexchange.com

**Bretzels**
Any kiosk

**Cinnamon buns**
Zeit für Brot
www.zeitfuerbrot.com

**Soluna Brot und Öl**
Gneisenaustr. 58,
Kreuzberg, 10961

**Italian bakery**
Sironi (in Markthalle Neun #36)
FB: sironi.de

**Austrian bakery**
Wiener Brot
www.wienerbrot.de

# 8    9    10

## Late Night Parties

**Watergate**
www.water-gate.de

**Kater Holzig**
www.katerholzig.de

**Tresor**
tresorberlin.com

**Berghain / Panorama Bar (#49)**
tresorberlin.com

**Suicide Circus**
www.suicide-berlin.com

**Weekend**
www.week-end-berlin.de

**Arena**
www.arena-berlin.de

**Chalet**
www.chalet-berlin.de

**Kjosk**
www.kjosk.com

## Leisure

**Hang out in front of a "Späti (late shops)"**
*Friedrichshain*

**Make a city trip on a boat**
count the bridges over Spree river

**Walk in Schöneberger Südgelände**
Railroad & industrial site buried in jungle

**Bath and relax**
Liquidrom
liquidrom-berlin.de

**Have summer picnic**
at one of the lakes or go find a derelict observatory or a forest

## Mementos

**4-strip black-and-white passport photo**
photoautomat
www.photoautomat.de

**Honey & Seed**
Prinzessinnengarten
prinzessinnengarten.net

**Crafted vodka**
Our/Berlin
Am Flutgraben 2,
Alt-Treptow, 12435

**Vintage German furniture**
*Rosenthaler pl. / Schönhauser allee (Mitte)*

**Berlin city map 1948**
Berliner Geschichtswerkstatt
www.berliner-geschichtswerkstatt.de

## Icon Index

 Opening hours

 Address

 Contact

Remarks

 Admission

 Facebook

 Website

 Scan QR codes to access Google Maps and discover the area around each destination. Internet connection required.

# 60x60

60 Local Creatives x 60 Hotspots

From vast cityscapes to the smallest snippets of conversation, there is much to inspire creative urges in Berlin. 60x60 points you to 60 haunts where 60 arbiters of taste develop their nose for the good stuff.

## Landmarks & Architecture
SPOTS · 01 – 12

Walk through history as you wander the veins of the city. Memorials, converted buildings and abandoned sites await to reveal the past with present-day reverence.

## Cultural & Art Space
SPOTS · 13 – 24

The city itself appears like a gallery space turned inside out, but do seek art and subculture hiding inside unconventional spaces, say bunkers, converted churches and sea cans.

## Markets & Shops
SPOTS · 25 – 36

Flea markets are a treasure hunter's bounty and offer a good view of local life, but if you opt for new designs check concept stores that have global picks and extensive choices.

## Restaurants & Cafés
SPOTS · 37 – 48

German classics will more than whet your appetite, but save quota for Berlin's universal culinary scene. Italian cooking and Korean kimchi are high quality and plentiful.

## Nightlife
SPOTS · 49 – 60

Choices seem to multiply daily. Will you watch a show in a swimming pool, do a beer tasting at a micro-brewery or get crazy in an underground techno club.

# Landmarks & Architecture

Epic architecture, Bauhaus ideologies and abandoned sites

Berlin's landmarks and architecture inevitably note its eventful history. Having been one of the major battlegrounds during the Second World War and Cold War divisions, the city of Berlin remains physically on the mend decades after the combat. Bullet marks and military infrastructure are still visible throughout the city, as new constructions restore the city's former glory and forge a new identity. Take a look back through history by visiting the numerous museums and historical remains. Holocaust Mahnmal (*Cora-Berliner-Str. 1, Mitte, 10117*) commemorates the murdered Jews, the Jewish Museum Berlin (*Lindenstr. 9-14, Kreuzburg, 10969*) documents Jewish life in East Germany, the rise and fall of Nazi government can be sighted at Topography of Terror (*Niederkirchnerstr. 8, Kreuzburg, 10963*), the old Tempelhof airport (#7), Teufelsberg (#10) and the Soviet War Memorial (#1) in Treptower Park. Although not the founding place of Bauhaus, the city still accommodates some of the earlier examples of the school, like Gropiusstadt (#6) conceptualised by Walter Gropius, and New National Gallery (*Potsdamer Str. 50, Tiergarten, 10785*) built by Ludwig Mies van der Rohe. More recent landmarks include the postwar reconstructions at Neues Museum (#13) completed in 2009 by David Chipperfield. Berlin TV tower (*Panoramastr. 1A, Mitte, 10178*) by Hermann Henselmann allows you a 360°C view of the city.

# 60X60 : LANDMARKS & ARCHITECTURE

**Azar Kazimir**
*Designer, Michelberger Hotel*

A graphic designer and illustrator from London, and Creative Director of Michelberger Hotel.

Spreepark
P.015

**Jan Paul Herzer**
*Sound artist, hands on sound*

I do things with sound and I run a small company, hands on sound. While being generally curious about sound and art, I specialise in acoustic scenography and interactive audio.

**Martin Niklas Wieser**
*Fashion designer*

I'm a fashion designer based in Berlin. I run a unisex collection that incorporates sportswear details into more classical wear.

Sowjetisches
Ehrenmal
P.014

Bauhaus-
Archiv
P.016

**Pret A Diner**
*Food & design event organiser*

Pret a Diner started with a notion to push the boundaries of dining experience and design. Behind the project are veteran caterer KP Kofler from Kofler & Kompanie and artist Olivia Steele.

Corbusier-
haus
P.018

**Enrico Bonafede**
*Graphic designer, Mjölk*

I am an Italian graphic designer who have been in Berlin since 2010. I love cooking and I'm a fanatic collector of old design books, vinyl and city maps.

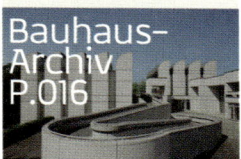

**A Nice Idea Every Day**
*Music video directors*

We are Vivien Weyrauch and Fabian Röttger, music video directors operating under the name A Nice Idea Every Day.

Deutsches
Historisches
Museum
P.017

Gropiusstadt
P.019

012

**Lisa Rienermann**
*Artist*

I am an author working in the wide field of illustration, photography, graphic design, bad spelling and concept. I like to explain words in pictures.

Caroline-von-Humboldt-Weg
P.022

**Eyal Burstein**
*Artist*

I was born in Tel Aviv, raised in London and am now based in Berlin. My work is a symbiosis of art and design resulting from long-term research, including my recent book *Taxing Art* (2011).

**Studio Laucke Siebein**
*Creative agency*

Studio Laucke Siebein has offices in Amsterdam and Berlin managed by partners Dirk Laucke and Johanna Siebein. We focus on creative strategies, identities and book design.

Tempelhofer Freiheit
P.020

Shell-Haus
P.023

**ICE CREAM FOR FREE™**
*Artist*

My name is Oliver Wiegner and I've been running the design and illustration studio ICE CREAM FOR FREE™ in Kreuzberg, Berlin, since 2005.

Berliner Unterwelten
P.026

**Daniel Bolliger**
*Fashion photographer*

I'm fashion photographer and art director from Switzerland but I do most of my productions in Berlin. Currently I live in NYC but I think Berlin is the most exciting city next to Tokyo.

**Florian Bayer**
*Illustrator & publisher*

I live and work between the borders of Kreuzberg and Neukölln. Besides being an illustrator, I'm the editor of *Shake Your Tree Edition* and run zine-press Naives and Visionaries.

Teufelsberg
P.024

Schwerbelastungskörper
P.027

## 1. Sowjetisches Ehrenmal
*Map M, P.110*

Lying peacefully at the heart of Treptower Park, the Soviet War Memorial serves both as a military cemetery and a monument commemorating 5,000 Soviet soldiers who died fighting Nazis in the Battle of Berlin in WWII. The centrepiece of the epic architecture is a 12-metre bronze Red Army soldier holding a rescued German child while crushing a swastika with his sword. Sixteen sarcophagi flank the compound's central avenue, impressing the weight of history on visitors. Each is etched with a Joseph Stalin quote, in Russian on one side of the walk, and German on the other.

🏠 *Treptower Park, Alt-Treptow, 12435*

*"Get a feeling of history here. Somehow this place isn't widely known, so you can often have it all to yourself."*

– Azar Kazimir, Michelberger Hotel

## 2  Spreepark
*Map M, P.110*

Forced to shut down in 2001 due to insolvency, Spreepark, known as Kulturpark Plänterwald before 1989's reunification, was East Germany's only permanent amusement park, and opened in 1969. For over a decade the fairground has sat silent leaving old rides and attractions to rust and slip into decay. Many seek a gap in the badly repaired fence and sneak in, but visitors can also walk in at weekends as the park owner's daughter runs her little café near the park's entrance and re-starts the mini-train on sunshiny days, charging a small fee for a ride. Sign up for a tour if you wish to learn the site's secret stories.

- 1100–1800 (Sa–Su, opening hours vary with season)
- Kiehnwerder Allee 1, Plänterwald, 12437
- www.berliner-spreepark.de
- Guided tour: €15, online booking only

*"The old fun rides and attractions are still there but are slowly falling apart. The whole area oozes a weird but inspiring atmosphere."*
– Jan Paul Herzer, hands on sound

## 60X60 : LANDMARKS & ARCHITECTURE

### 3. Bauhaus-Archiv
*Map G, P.107*

The school of Bauhaus fundamentally influenced German aesthetics and is seen to stand for modernity, diversity and tolerance around the world. Despite the school's closure in 1933 under the Nazi regime, the movement continued with the school founder Walter Gropius initiating a documentation of Bauhaus ideology and influences in 1964. Today, the Gropius-built museum holds the world's largest and most comprehensive collection of original drawings, sculptures and models as well as furniture, metalwork, photography and stage pieces composed by Bauhaus masters and students. In cooperation with art:berlin, the archive organises tours to visit important examples of modern architecture in Berlin and environs.

- 1000–1700 (W-M)
- €7/4 (Sa-M), €6/3 (W-F)
- Klingelhöferstr. 14, Tiergarten, 10785
- +49 (0)30 25 40 020
- www.bauhaus.de

*"A true landmark to Berlin."*
– Martin Niklas Wieser

### 4. Deutsches Historisches Museum
*Map E, P.105*

Lodged inside a 18th-century *zeughaus* (armoury), the German Historical Museum chronicles the country's history in a breadth of daily objects and visual arts. The adjacent exhibition hall stands in stark relief against baroque-style architecture, with a glass-walled foyer and a spiral staircase – extensions added after the museum's major renovation (1994–8) and the only work by I. M. Pei. in Berlin. Access the museum at Hinter dem Gießhaus 3, or via Schlüterhof, an inner courtyard with glass roofing by Andreas Schlüter (1664–1714).

🕐 1000–1800 daily  💲 €8/4
📍 Unter den Linden 2, Mitte, 10117
📞 +49 (0)30 20 30 40
🔗 www.dhm.de

*"It's one of our exclusive catering locations in Berlin!"*
— Pret A Diner

## 5 Corbusierhaus
Map N, P.111

Named after the architect Le Corbusier (1887–1965), Corbusierhaus was the third in a series of large-scale settlements built for the displaced after WWII (The Unitè d'Habitation in Marseilles, France that Le Corbusier completed in 1952, was the first). Its success has inspired continual implementation of the social housing model, a "vertical villa" considering both individual and communal space, although German regulations has forced the Berliner edition to increase the floor height, inevitably resulting in excessive sunlight to the 530 flats. Corbusierhaus was also part of the International Building Exhibition in 1957.

Flatowallee 16, Charlottenburg, 14055
www.corbusierhaus-berlin.de
Guided tour: corbusierhaus-berlin.org, €5

"A modular utopia. Corbusierhaus and the Hansaviertel locality in Tiergarten are both the finest examples of 1960s Modern architecture."
– Enrico Bonafede, Mjölk

## 6 Gropiusstadt
Map O, P.111

"Light, air and sun" was a slogan for idealised public housing developments in the early 1960s. As the city's first major settlement, Gropiusstadt was seen as a social utopia as imagined by Bauhaus founder Walter Gropius (1883–1969). Central heating, shopping centres, schools and community centres brought urban convenience and modern living to Neukölln's southern fringe, although Gropius' original design has since been modified. The erection of the Berlin Wall in 1961 restricted the site and squeezed building height to a maximum of 30 storeys. The project was completed in 1975, six years after Gropius' death.

🏠 Neukölln, 12353
🔗 www.qm-gropiusstadt.de

*"Plain crazy, mysterious, scary, beautiful and unlike the rest of Berlin. The 30th floor has the best view all over Berlin."*

– A Nice Idea Every Day

60X60 : **LANDMARKS & ARCHITECTURE**

### 7  Tempelhofer Freiheit
*Map K, P.108*

Tempelhofer Freiheit was one of the world's first airports, with a terminal building that displays a classic example of Nazi architecture. It was at once a symbol of Nazi regime, where concentration camp prisoners were forced to assemble bombers during WWII; and freedom, as gateway to flee Soviet East Germany during the Berlin blockade for 11 months. Tempelhof airport operated until 2008. The grounds are now used as a public park with the city's panorama view as the backdrop.

- Dawn till dusk daily  €13/9/7
- Pl. der Luftbrücke 5, Tempelhofer-Schöeberg, 12107
- www.tempelhoferfreiheit.de
- Guided tour: 1500 (Sa), 1400 (Su)

*"If you want BBQ, there are three designated areas that get crowded quickly. You can sit almost everywhere for a picnic and have loads of space for yourself."*
– Lisa Rienermann

60X60 : LANDMARKS & ARCHITECTURE

## 8. Caroline-von-Humboldt-Weg
*Map C, P.103*

Colourfully aligned on Caroline-von-Humboldt-Weg, this collection of characterful townhouses are the result of the Berlin Senate's intention to realise people's aspirations to own their own houses. The initial idea was to keep the total cost of building a home with a gross floor area of around 450 sqm to less than one million euros. The commissioning of private building contractors led to the area's distinctive individuality, conjuring up a modern village within the German capital's heart. The noble project, however, did not expand within the city due to the lack of sites, but has set an example for other cities' planning.

🏠 *Caroline-von-Humboldt-Weg, Mitte, 10117*

*"The townhouses were built from 2005 to 2008. The newly developed street was the former site of the Reichsbank destroyed in WWII."*

– Eyal Burstein

### 9 Shell-Haus
*Map G, P.107*

Slender ribbon windows flow with the wave on the undulating façade at Shell-Haus, designed by German architect and professor Emil Fahrenkamp (1885–1966). The building projects a Modernist statement over the Landwehr Canal. Taking only two years to complete, in 1931, the office block was a surprise in many ways, from small details like bespoke window handles to technological innovations like air vents built beneath the sidewalk, reducing the impact of ground vibrations on the steel-framed high-rise. The building has received extensive restoration, beginning after WWII until today.

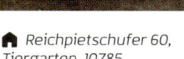
Reichpietschufer 60, Tiergarten, 10785
www.shell-haus.com

> "What I like most is that the building's two- and three-dimensional effect is cheating you constantly. Do approach it from different angles."
> – Studio Laucke Siebein

60X60 : **LANDMARKS & ARCHITECTURE**

### 10 Teufelsberg
*Map P, P.111*

Literally and atmospherically a "Devil's Mountain," Teufelsberg is a man-made hill heaped up as the city started to rebuild after WWII. But there is not only war rubble. Buried deep beneath the 120-metre mound is a never-finished Nazi military college. Since then, Teufelsberg was also taken as the US listening station used by the NSA during Cold War, then built into a never-used luxury hotel-apartment complex before the developer ran into deep debts, and Hollywood director David Lynch flagged it as a desirable site for his meditation school. Wear sturdy shoes to enter. On Sundays in the warmer months, you'll find hundreds of people flying kites and paragliding on site.

- 1200-1800 hourly & daily
- €7
- Teufelsseechaußee 10, Wilmersdorf, 14193
- www.berlinsightout.de
- Guided tour: 1300 (Sa-Su), €15/8, 18+

*"It's a part of Berlin's Grunewald Forest, housing strange looking buildings with interesting stories."*
– ICE CREAM FOR FREE™

## 11 Berliner Unterwelten

Map I, P.108

This former bunker underneath U-Bahn station Gesundbrunnen is one of many subterranean labyrinths that contain bomb-raid shelters, ammunition stores and prison escape tunnels that connect via the city's subway network. Alongside it runs a historic pneumatic system – 400 kilometres of tubes once used to deliver mail by pressurised air, in use until 1976. Guided tours are available all year with tickets sold on the day from a pavilion next to Gesundbrunnen station's south entrance, starting from around 10am.

*Tour schedule & admission vary with themes*
Brunnenstr. 105, Wedding, 13355
+49 (0)30 49 91 05 17
berliner-unterwelten.de

*"It is breathtaking to see and feel the energy of this dark underground world. Definitely need to book a tour. A must see."*
– Daniel Bolliger

## 12 Schwerbelastungskörper
*Map H, P.107*

This huge concrete cylinder is another relic from the Nazi era, and demonstrates the power Hitler wished to execute through massive structures. The project was headed by Hitler's chief architect Albert Speer (1905–81), with visions of building two highways that would have intersected in the "world capital," with a gigantic triumphal arch at the end of the North–South route. The "Heavy Load-Bearing Body," as its German name denotes, was a 12,650-tonne load-bearing tester for the arch and was still in its planning stage when WWII stalled the build. The structure was listed as a historic monument in 1995.

🕒 Apr–Oct: 1400–1800 (Tu–W), 1000– (Sa), 1300–1600 (Su)
🏠 General-Pape-Str., Tempelhofer-Schöeberg, 12101
🔗 www.schwerbelastungskoerper.de
🎫 Guided tour: Berliner Unterwelten (#11), Tour S, €6

*"It's a very weird kind of architecture, built in very weird times by very weird people to test some very weird plans."*
– Florian Bayer

# Cultural & Art Space

Urban art, young galleries and private initiatives

Berlin allows a kind of creative freedom hardly found anywhere else. The resulting diversified cultural scene has attracted countless artists, designers and gallerists and every type of art, in intercrossing disciplines from food and fashion to music and publishing, all found in the German capital. Streets like Revaler Straße (#21) make for an open-air gallery for urban artists like Evol, Blu and Vhils, while new and more established galleries are settling in Potsdamer Straße and the neighbourhood of Mitte, including Museum Island, which was added to the UNESCO list of World Heritage Sites in 1999. Take the chance to visit independent initiatives, such as the KW Institute for Contemporary Art (#17) and Museum of Letters (#19), which is set up to preserve signs and letterforms. The Boros Collection (#22) of privately-held contemporary art can be reckoned as one of a kind, sitting inside a converted bunker where its founder, Christian Boros and his family reside. Those wanting to sample the perfect acoustics and atmospheric chamber music made popular in 19th century Europe should head to Clärchens Ballhaus' Mirror Hall (#46). Seek out dinner presentations where delicious feasts are served alongside a wonderful programme.

60X60 : CULTURAL & ART SPACE

**Sissi Goetze**
*Fashion designer*

My name is Sissi Goetze. I graduated with an MA in menswear from Central Saint Martins College London in 2010. After moving back to Berlin I started my own label in 2011.

## Bode-Museum P.033

**ZWEIDREI**
*Multidisciplinary artist*

Architect and young urban professional. Radical conservative punks with Molotov and a tie.

**Jeongmoon Choi**
*Artist*

I am a Korean artist spliting time between Berlin and Seoul. I like to travel in big cities to enjoy different architecture, people and good food.

## Neues Museum P.032

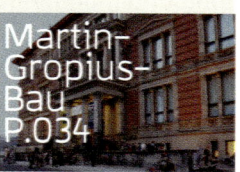

## Martin-Gropius-Bau P.034

**Raban Ruddigkeit**
*Art director, + Ruddigkeit*

I was born in Leipzig, the city of books, in 1968. I'm also the founder of "Freistil – Best of European Commercial Illustration" and co-editor of "Typodarium" and "Poladarium".

## Kunstwerke Berlin P.037

**Tino Seubert**
*Product designer*

I was born in Germany and studied design in Italy, France and the UK. My work bridges various visual disciplines and resonates with historical references to places and materials.

**Maiko Gubler**
*Visual artist*

I work with digital modeling tools in imagery and sculpture. I'm interested in the indefiniteness of mixed realities and I'm compelled to embrace the virtual as actual.

## PLATOON KUNSTHALLE Berlin P.036

## abc Art Berlin Contemporary P.038

**Potipoti**
*Fashion label & boutique*

Potipoti was founded in 2005 as a collaboration between two designers, Silvia Salvador and Nando Cornejo. Our philosophy is to bridge the gap between graphic design, art and fashion.

ST. AGNES
P.042

**Li Wolfgang Schiffer**
*Advertising director & agent*

I am originally from Korea and now work as an advertising film director in Berlin. Besides directing I represent the amazingly talented people of Woodblock and Celluloid VFX.

**Ben & Julia**
*Film & art director duo*

Benoit Créac'h and Julia Gaudard joined forces in 2006 to become today's Ben & Julia. The French-Swiss duo create through puppetry, 2D and 3D animation and live action.

Buchstaben-
museum
P.040

Revaler
Straße
P.043

**Our/Berlin**
*Micro-distillery*

Our/Berlin is a micro-volka-distillery run by Paul Sanders (Pauline Hoch and Jon D. Sanders), in hands with Pernod Ricard Global. Our/Berlin produces Our/Vodka in the heart of Berlin.

Ehemalige
Jüdische
Mädchen-
schule
P.046

**Nicky&Max**
*Photographer & food stylist*

We met a few years ago and created our own food blog devoted to food photography. Nicky is British and came here from London a few years ago. Max is a native Berliner.

**Timo Gaessner**
*Designer, 123buero*

Timo Gaessner studied at the Gerrit Rietveld Academie in Amsterdam and founded 123buero in 2002. He also runs an independent press MilieuGrotesque focusing on type design.

Sammlung
Boros
P.044

Galerie
Thomas
Fischer
P.047

### Neues Museum
Map E, P.105

Badly bombed in WWII and left in ruins for more than 60 years, the New Museum was originally designed by Friedrich August Stüler (1800-65) and built between 1843 and 1855. It reopened in 2009 after a thorough restoration. The restoration, overseen by David Chipperfield Architects, was said to have successfully given the building a new soul without imitating what was lost, and won the architect the Mies van der Rohe 2011 award. Currently on permanent display are the museum's Egyptian Museum and Papyrus Collection, the Museum of Prehistory and Early History and various artefacts from the Collection of Classical Antiquities.

🕐 1000-1800 (F-W), -2000 (Th)   💲 €12/11
🏠 Bodestr. 1-3, Museumsinsel, 10178   📞 +49 (0)30 26 64 24 242   🌐 www.neues-museum.de

"*An amazing reconstruction of the classical building, where powerful new parts blend in impressively with the preserved original parts of the building.*"
– Sissi Goetze

## 14 Bode-Museum
*Map E, P.105*

The Baroque Bode, with its iconic dome, was built at the northern tip of Museum Island in the early 20th century, and like much of the city faced bombing during the Second World War. The Bode reopened following an extensive nine-year restoration in 2006, with a new Byzantine focus. Presented are sculpture and art treasures ranging in date from the early Middle Ages to the Renaissance. Check out the antique and secondhand book market held on Am Kupfergraben next to the museum's entrance. It takes place most weekends and some holidays from 11am to 5pm.

- 1000-1800 (Tu-Su), -2000 (Th)
- €8/7  Am Kupfergraben, Museumsinsel 10117
- +49 (0)30 26 64 24 242
- bodemuseum

*"Best classical sculpture collection in town."*
— ZWEIDREI

60X60 : **CULTURAL & ART SPACE**

### 15 Martin-Gropius-Bau
Map G, P.107

A magnificent building with combined classical and Renaissance features built by architects Martin Gropius (1824–80, a great uncle of Walter Gropius) and Heino Schmieden (1835–1913). Gropius Bau today is a much-loved venue for cultural festivals and exhibitions of contemporary art. Severely damaged near the end of WWII but restored in the 1970s, the listed building also celebrates German theatre with the annual Theatertreffen festival, and music, hosting MaerzMusik (spring), Musikfest Berlin (fall) and Jazzfest Berlin (fall) festivals.

🕙 1000-1900 (W-M)  💲 Ticket price varies with event  🏠 Niederkirchnerstr. 7, Kreuzberg, 10963  📞 +49 (0)30 25 48 60  🌐 www.gropiusbau.de

"*Better visit as early as possible. It gets more crowded after midday.*"
– Jeongmoon Choi

035

## 60X60 : CULTURAL & ART SPACE

### 16 PLATOON KUNSTHALLE Berlin
*Map E, P.105*

Thirty-four assembled cargo canisters offer an unusual urban playground at Platoon's. With cultural and residency programmes curated by Platoon themselves as well as guest curators, the modular architecture is a dynamic space for ideas to be tested. Experimental creations are also put on public display, provoking discussion on street, music, media, design and the video arts. On the regular lineup are party-like monthly vintage fashion fairs and Donnerstagsbar party nights on Thursdays. Small scale performances usually start at 9pm till late.

- 0900-0000 daily
- Schönhauser allee 9, Prenzlauer Berg, 10119
- +49 (0)30 28 88 21 60
- www.kunsthalle.com/berlin

"A 'must see' among the boring architecture of Mitte. Just pass by. There's always something going on."
– Raban Ruddigkeit, + Ruddigkeit

### 17. Kunstwerke Berlin
*Map E, P.105*

An independent institution founded in the early 1990s by a group of young individuals and Klaus Biesenbach, Director of MoMA PS1, New York, KW always has a programme of contemporary art exhibitions with bright young artists and leading institutions. It has also initiated the Berlin Biennale for contemporary art, which hosts its eighth edition in 2014. Alongside, a library, a bookshop and a walk-in art piece imagined by artist Dan Graham and realised with architect Johanne Nalbach as Café Bravo, FEED Soundspace at KW has a lineup of interactive discussions and concerts focusing on sound art.

- 1200–1900 (W–M), –2100 (Th)  €6/4
- Auguststr. 69, Mitte, 10117
- +49 (0)30 24 34 590
- www.kw-berlin.de, FEED: www.6554.de

*"Kunstwerke always shows well-curated exhibitions with often young artists. Their shows haven't been shown in ten other big museums around the world!"*

– Tino Seubert

60X60 : CULTURAL & ART SPACE

## 18 abc Art Berlin Contemporary

In 2008, nine galleries decided to join forces and launch the debut edition of abc, bringing an artist-centred approach to its shows. Today the movement has become an eagerly awaited annual art festival. Growing number of galleries partake in the event, with up to a hundred art projects, including premier and site-specific works, responding to a yearly theme. Berlin Art Week and Berlin Art Book Fair have also presented recent editions. Additional lectures and special performances by appearing artists are a regular staple.

Mid-September annually, Opening hour, ticket price & venue vary with year
www.artberlincontemporary.com

"The abc fair has my favourite galleries: Kraupa-Tuskany Zeidler, Tanya Leighton, Galerie Thomas Fischer, Société and, hopefully soon, the marvelous Future Gallery!"
– Maiko Gubler

### 19 **Buchstabenmuseum**
*Map A, P.102*

Type and logo addicts will be happy to find out the genre has a home in Berlin. Started by Barbara Dechant and Anja Schulze in 2005 as a private collection, the Museum of Letters is an initiative that rescues, restores and documents the story of signage, primarily with acrylic and metal logotypes, and that once individualised businesses from train stations to the local fishmonger. As a self-sustaining project the museum leads a nomadic life, moving whenever rents rise. Patron visits help keep this mission alive.

- 1300–1700 (Th–Su)　€6.50/3.50
- Holzmarktstr. 66, Mitte, 10179
- +49 (0)17 74 20 15 87
- www.buchstabenmuseum.de
- Guided tour: €35 (flat rate for 1–25 individuals), appointment required, Cash only

*"Taking pictures in the museum and making sentences with the letters are the favourite things we do. It's our favourite 'hidden' museum in Berlin!"*
– Potipoti

60X60 : **CULTURAL & ART SPACE**

## ST. AGNES
*Map D, P.103*

A once-sacred institution for God is due to become a temple of arts. Built by Werner Düttmann (1921-83) in 1967 for the war-destructed neighbourhood, the Brutalist structure was particularly designed for social purpose, with raw concrete structures and brick rubble. Demolition was initially arranged due its low utility rate, but was later replaced with a re-construction plan, overseen by architect Arno Brandlhuber, which involves converting the skylit chapel into a new home for the Johann König Gallery. ST. AGNES is closed for renovation work until 2014 fall.

- *Opening hours vary with event*
- *Alexandrinenstr. 118-121, Kreuzberg, 10969*
- *+49 (0)30 26 10 30 80*
- *www.st-agnes.net*

*"A 'must see' for all art and architecture lovers."*
– Li Wolfgang Schiffer

## 21 Revaler Straße
*Map A, P.103*

Stretching 1.2km along the neighbourhood Friedrichshain, Revaler Straße is home to Berlin's underground landmarks, derelict factories and street art. Well-known artists like Italian-born Blu left massive drawings, after repeatedly painting and erasing his world-famous time-lapse clips. An urban art mural itself, the century-old building at No.99 is a complex with art gallery, vegetarian kitchen, and a techno club. Wrap up your day with a walk to Modersohn-Brücke (Modersohnstr.). If you are lucky, in summer, there will be people dancing until the sun sets.

*Friedrichshain, 10245*

*"Go there on Sunday for the flea market at RAW (Revaler Straße 99, 9am-5pm)."*

– Ben & Julia

###  Sammlung Boros
*Map E, P.104*

Comprising spectacular works of contemporary art dating from 1990 to the present, the Boros Collection is open for public view in a revitalised bunker, owned by private art collector and ad agency owner Christian Boros and his wife. The couple also curates the shows, which encompass all media, from sculptures to drawings, installations and photography. Right after the first edition (2008-12), the second (2012-) now awaits visitors to roam over the 3,000 sqm space and 80 rooms, with sound installations and artwork by artists including Ai Weiwei, Olafur Eliasson and Wolfgang Tillmans. The Boros family live atop the bunker in a penthouse designed by Jens Casper.

- Th-Su
- €12/6
- Reinhardtstr. 20, Mitte, 10117
- info@sammlung-boros.de
- www.sammlung-boros.de
- By guided tour only, appointment required

*"Gallery with a great selection of contemporary art. Book a guided tour 1-2 months in advance."*
– Our/Berlin

60X60 : CULTURAL & ART SPACE

##  Ehemalige Jüdische Mädchenschule
*Map E, P.105*

Exquisite architecture by the then prominent Jewish architect Alexander Beer (1873-1944), interiors and rooftop garden hint at this Jewish girls' school's illustrious past. After its closure in 1942 by the Nazi's, the school was only officially returned to the Jewish community in 2009, and today houses two excellent restaurants, the second largest Kennedy museum and four galleries. Tenants include gallerist Michael Fuchs who proposed the conversion.

- Opening hours vary with galleries
- Auguststr. 11-13, Mitte, 10117
- +49 (0)30 33 00 60 70
- www.maedchenschule.org

*"The Pastrami Sandwich in Mogg and Melzer, the Jewish Delicatessen, is worth the visit alone. Arrive before noon to secure a table."*

– Nicky&Max

### 24  Galerie Thomas Fischer
*Map G, P.107*

There's plenty of galleries to be seen in this district. Highly recommended is Galerie Thomas Fischer. Climb the curved staircase up to the gallery to be brought face to face with the latest in whatever ambitious exhibition founder and fervent conceptual art advocate, Thomas Fischer is presenting. At No.50, Neue Nationalgalerie always has great programmes within a beautiful building and with a sculptural garden designed by Ludwig Mies van der Rohe (1886–1969).

- 1100-1800 (Tu-Sa)
- 1F, Haus H, Potsdamer Str. 77-87, Schöneberg, 10785
- +49 (0)30 74 78 03 85
- www.galeriethomasfischer.de

*"Try to get into a conversation with the owners and discuss their show."*

– Timo Gaessner, 123buero

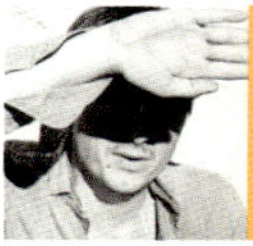

# Markets & Shops

Flea markets, art bookshops and concept stores

Berlin has become the quintessential capital of vintage. Antiques, books, secondhand, music, handicrafts, vintage postcards and bespoke letterpressed business cards can be found in different flea markets across the city. Check this section and in *Count to 10* for highlights. Equally great in amount is the varied, independent art bookshops. Locals keep their fingers on the pulse visiting these dens of artistic information on a regular basis. Tap into the culture yourself with a visit or two. Stores include RAUM Italic (#27) a publisher and design studio focused on the Italian art scene, as well as those offering libraries of niche, rare or out-of-print books. Check listings and events, as most schedule exhibitions, talks, forums and launches. For a more comprehensive view of local life, Manufactum (#31) stocks sophisticated housewares and stationery that are often locally made. Concept stores like Andreas Murkudis (#26), VooStore (#25) and Quartier 206 department store (#30) are where you can shop for local couture and designer clothes, with Dudes Factory (#32) offering graphic design products and Süper Store (#28) curated selections of unique home accessories.

## 60X60 : MARKETS & SHOPS

**Sigurd Larsen**
*Architect*

I'm a Danish architect working across the fields of architecture, design and art. My work combines the aesthetics of quality materials with concepts focusing on functionality in complex spaces.

### VooStore
### P.052

### Andreas Murkudis
### P.054

**Mark Braun**
*Industrial designer*

I run a studio in Berlin where I realise quality designs of furniture and fixtures for the like of Authentics and Lobmeyr. My studio editions have been shown at galleries like Saatchi.

**Robert Hanson**
*Illustrator*

I am a freelance illustrator from the UK and have been living in Berlin for the past five years.

### RAUM Italic (SPAZIO Corsivo)
### P.055

**Judith Seng**
*Artist*

I investigate our contemporary culture and its materialised manifestations. My work spans the field between research, experimentation and creation of objects and spaces.

### Süper Store
### P.056

### Motto Berlin
### P.057

**Eva Gonçalves**
*Designer, Unfinished Inventory*

Eva Gonçalves is a Portuguese communication designer, researcher and writer. I co-founded Salon Renate with a couple of friends and design blog, We Celebrate.

**Michael Sontag**
*Fashion designer*

I blur the common fashion borders and create a generality detached from fashion parameters such as seasons, trends and consumer ages.

### Quartier 206
### P.058

**Ryu Itadani**
*Artist*

My name is Ryu Itadani. I am a painter. City, things and nature are the theme for my artwork. I see the lines first, then I see the colours.

Dudes Factory
P.060

**Guillaume Kashima**
*Artist*

I've lived here for six years. I used to like the energy of the club scene but as I got older, I play it low-profile and cool at the places I recommend here.

**Michael Rosen**
*Curator*

Through my agency Digital in Berlin (D/B), I develop, curate and present unique event concepts and concerts around the world.

Manufactum
P.059

Nowkölln Flowmarkt
P.061

**Björn Andersson**
*Product designer*

After working as a design architect in NYC, Stockholm and Shanghai for 10 years, I opened Björn Andersson Studio in Berlin. My work was exhibited at DMY (Berlin) and LDW 2013 (London).

Flohmarkt Friedrichshagen
P.064

**Siriusmo**
*Musician*

I am Siriusmo. I produce interessting electronic music! ; )

**Veronika Wildgruber**
*Eyewear designer*

I studied product design in Italy, and worked in Paris and London for years afterwards. In 2011 I founded my own practice, Veronika Wildgruber Eyewear in Berlin.

Trödelmarkt Arkonaplatz
P.062

Markthalle Neun
P.065

# 60X60 : MARKETS & SHOPS

## 25  VooStore
*Map A, P.102*

Despite a quiet air of secrecy, good things hide among the little courtyards nestled in the decaying establishments along Oranienstraße. Among them, snuggled inside a former locksmith shop, VooStore exudes a wholesome atmosphere with fancy selections of high fashion and streetwear, a small cafè (#38) and a decent magazine department housed in an artfully vintage interior (with good-looking staff to boot). After filling your shopping bag, head over to the courtyard building at No.25. On the third floor, lesser-known Museum der Dinge (Museum of Things) is an interesting showcase of everyday life.

- 1100–2000 (M-Sa)
- Oranienstr. 24, Kreuzberg, 10999
- +49 (0)30 61 65 11 19
- www.vooberlin.com

*"Our furniture is exhibited and sold from the store. They have the best coffee in Kreuzberg."*

– Sigurd Larsen

### Andreas Murkudis
Map G, P.107

Perhaps more a gallery than a clothing retailer, entrepreneur and fashion label, Andreas Murkudi displays his taste for high-end fashion and living in his 1,000 sqm concept store, with lighting and furniture designed by German architect Gonzalez Haase. The white space is loosely zoned, and presents international designer labels, from high fashion items to ready-to-wear. Among the collections are pieces by the founder's fashion designer brother, Kostas Murkudis, alongside a curated collection of design objects, with homeware and products for children both showcased.

1000-2000 (M-Sa)
Potsdamer Str. 81E, Tiergarten, 10785  +49 (0)30 68 07 98 306
www.andreasmurkudis.com

"A 'must go' for every design and fashion interested person. Andreas Murkudis is a unique store for exclusive goods and rare clothing."
– Mark Braun

### 27 RAUM Italic (SPAZIO Corsivo)
Map B, P.103

Tucked in a quiet little street at the fringe of Prenzlauer Berg, a hippy district of independent galleries and shops, bookshop RAUM Italic draws artists and designers sharing a love for Italian art and design. A partner and distributor of Italian independent press Corraini Edizioni, their offering also includes in-house publications alongside zines, fiction and nonfiction published by the likes of BOLO Paper (Italy) and Lars Müller (Switzerland). Keep up with their website for chances to meet new artists, or news of book presentations and exhibitions.

- 1200-1900 (M), 1000- (Tu-Sa)
- Schliemannstr. 29, Prenzlauer Berg, 10437
- +49 (0)30 94 05 76 65
- www.raumitalic.com

*"It has my favourite selection of design and illustration books – many of which are unexpected and things I haven't seen elsewhere."*

– Robert Hanson

### 28 Süper Store
Map L, P.109

As its name suggests, this place offers a *super* range of quirky finds for creating a sweet and sophisticated home. From the elegant stork-shaped scissors of 19th-century midwives to ornate Turkish copper bowls, dedicate wood toys to Süper's own brand of tote bags, the catalogue here articulates a quest for simple, brilliant home concepts. Back-Art GbR Andreas und Cordelia Pfanner is an added extra. The little bakery next door bakes some of the city's best bagels and cakes!

🕐 1100-1900 (Tu-F), -1600 (Sa)
🏠 Dieffenbachstr. 12, Kreuzberg, 10967  ☎ +49 (0)30 98 32 79 44
URL www.sueper-store.de

*"A small shop that offers a nice selection of special items you'll love and want to have."*
– Judith Seng

### 29 Motto Berlin
Map A, P.102

A Mecca for artists, designers, independent publishers and collectors of printed matter, Motto sits hidden away from busy Skalitzer Straße in a former factory courtyard, but can fill quickly. Aside from stocking niche publications and magazines oft-overlooked by mainstream booksellers, the store runs a regular programme of book launches, readings, exhibitions and talks. The store specialises in works on art, photography, typography and graphic design.

- 1200-2000 (M-Sa)
- Skalitzer Str. 68, Kreuzberg, 10997
- +49 (0)30 48 81 64 07
- www.mottodistribution.com

"Make sure you visit Motto with plenty of time on your hands and a healthy budget. It's the perfect place to go and see what's happening in the current scene."

– Eva Gonçalves, Unfinished Inventory

60X60 : **MARKETS & SHOPS**

### 30 Quartier 206
*Map C, P.103*

Owner and interior designer Anne Maria Jagdfeld handpicks the catalogue for upscale mall Quartier 206. Pieces by fashion's brightest, such as Isabel Marant, Dries Van Noten and Manolo Blahnik are stocked among others. An amble around the glamorous interior reveals breathtaking Art-Deco-style interiors with marble-checkered floors and a star-shaped skylight by Pei, Cobb, Freed & Partners. A sub-terranean walkway leads to Galeries Lafayette with a Jean Nouvel glass funnel across the street, and Quartier 205 holding crushed car sculptures by John Chamberlain (1927-2011).

- 1100-2000 (M-F), 1000-1800 (Sa)
- Friedrichstr. 71, Mitte, 10117
- www.dsq206.com

"Berlin is the capital of vintage. But if you don't like vintage, just go to Quartier 206 and buy a piece of MICHAEL SONTAG. ; )"
–Michael Sontag

058

### 31 Manufactum
*Map J, P.108*

For writers, chefs, gardeners and bohemians clamoring for good design, traditional crafts and first-rate materials, Manufactum is heaven. The seven-storey warehouse at Ernst-Reuter-Platz is chock-full of extraordinary yet reasonably priced stationery, classic tools, household goods and toys meant to be a joy to see, use and touch. Budget to spend on a treasure hunt here and finish your trip at Brot & Butter next door. A part of the shop, this little bistro and bakery delivers beautifully home-baked bread, fresh coffee and light plates.

🕐 1000-2000 (M-F), -1800 (Sa)
🏠 Hardenbergerstr. 4-5, Charlottenburg, 10623
📞 +49 (0)30 24 03 38 44
🌐 www.manufactum.de

*"It is fun to walk around the shop. There are lots of 'Made in Germany' products there."*

– Ryu Itadani

60X60 : MARKETS & SHOPS

## 32 Dudes Factory
Map E, P.105

Dudes Factory is a brand of conviction with a penchant for fusing graphic art with everyday life. An elite network of artists, illustrators and designers, all distinct in their own creative style and attitude, work with the gallery and store, which regularly initiates themed artistic projects and realises them in a continuous flow of unusual products, men's and women's apparel and skateboard art. Artwork is released as woodprints, screenprints, digital prints or original prints. In-house digital printing means these souvenirs are all marked authentically 'Made in Berlin.'

- 1200-2000 (M-Sa)
- Torstr. 138, Mitte, 10119
- +49 (0)30 40 00 58 99
- www.dudes-factory.com

*"If you can't find anything good in the shop (which I doubt), go for made-to-order. Choose a print and come back for it later… Yes, like pizzas!"*
– Guillaume Kashima

### 33 Nowkölln Flowmarkt
Map L, P.109

Called "Nowkölln" for its location, where Kreuzberg and Neukölln overlap, this fortnightly summer event has quickly lured a loyal (and stylish) crowd to the banks of the Landwehr Canal. As vendors and young designers spread out unique offerings, commonly secondhand goodies, art, music and original handicrafts, a happy vibe pervades. Locals advise venturing out on a morning trip for rarer offerings and evenings for the best bargains. Afternoons offer great market food and live street music. This place is unbeatable in the warmer months.

- 1000-1800 (1st & 3rd Su except winter)
- Maybachufer 31, Neukölln, 12047
- www.nowkoelln.de

*"There's also a Turkish market nearby where you can find colourful vegetables and Turkish specialities. It opens on Tuesdays and Fridays 11am–6.30pm."*

– Michael Rosen

## 60X60 : MARKETS & SHOPS

### 34 Trödelmarkt Arkonaplatz
*Map E, P.105*

If the widely known Mauerpark Sunday market is a must-go destination for everything from clothing to outdoor karaoke, Arkonaplatz is the place to source "real deals." Small and not overrun, the friendly local marketplace offers a constantly updated stock of authentic vintage furniture, knickknacks from 1950s and 1960s and retro fashion pieces, in good, clean condition, and which surrounding shops would charge a fortune for. Come in the morning for a good buy, as prime picks get taken quick.

🕙 1000-1600 (Su, except P.H.)
📍 Arkonapl.atz, Kiez, 10435
🔗 www.troedelmarkt-arkonaplatz.de

---

"*Perfect for laid back vintage shopping, with nice cafés and ice-cream bars in the neighbourhood.*"

– Björn Andersson, Björn Andersson Studio

### 35 Flohmarkt Friedrichshagen
*Map F, P.106*

Berlin's flea markets always promise a little adventure, where a wander through the stalls offers one surprise after the next. Try making a short trip to Friedrichshagen and catch the art and antique market right next to S-Bahn station. On a Sunday morning the place is filled with more GDR-era relics and is less touristy than better known locales. Afterwards, walk five minutes down Bölschestraße to grab lunch at Die Spindel at No.51 which dishes out A-class food in this beautiful area. Otherwise, an alfresco lunch next to the enchanting Müggelsee lake makes for a perfect alternative.

🕐 0800–1600 (Su)
🏠 S-Bahnhof Friedrichshagen, Friedrichshagen, 12555

"Beside all the inner-city markets, this one is most interesting, filled with loot from people's cellars."
– Siriusmo

### 36  Markthalle Neun
Map A, P.102

After narrowly escaping conversion to a supermarket, in 2011, Markthalle Neun continues to be jam-packed with privately-owned bakeries, smokehouses, on-site breweries and canteens where farm-to-table chefs busy themselves between harvests, stove and customers – as it has done for the last 120 years. While the marketplace is lively on Fridays and Saturdays as farmers and purveyors congregate to trade fresh produce, cheeses, cured meats and cakes, Thursdays spark the wow factor. Arrive early to join a street food craze that sees a sprightly mix of professional and amateur cooks gather to serve dishes as diverse as traditional German food to vegan specialities.

🕐 Weekly market: 1000–1800 (F–Sa), Eateries: 1200–1600 (M–Sa), Street Food Thursday: 1700–2200 (Th)
🏠 Eisenbahnstr. 42/43, Kreuzberg, 10997  URL www.markthalleneun.de

*"Nice place to have lunch on Fridays and Saturdays, special food market on Thursday evenings. Local, organic food. Nice atmosphere."*

– Veronika Wildgruber

Bitte
AM TRESEN
bestellen

Öffnungszeiten
MON-FREI 8:30-19:00
SAT, SONN+FEIERTAGE
10:00-19:00

Gäste,
vom 24.
inklusive
unser Urlaub.
Wir wünschen Euch
einen guten Rutsch.

# Restaurants & Cafés

Specialty cafés, ethnic food and historic ballrooms

Berlin's rich immigrant history and continued appeal to global thinkers and college students inform deep gastronomic diversity. Turkish, Italians, Vietnamese and Koreans in the cultural capital have been steadily growing in numbers over the years, as do their restaurants. Both original fusion and home recipes add to the charm of Berlin's multicultural landscape. But German nourishment is irreplaceable, with sourdough bread, bretzels, currywurst, schnitzel and pork knuckle with sauerkraut remaining at the heart of national cuisine. Try Paul Saal when you visit Ehemalige Jüdische Mädchenschule (#23), Clärchens Ballhaus (#46) or Austria (*Bergmannstr. 30, Kreuzberg, 10961*) for a genuine taste of German food. When it comes to Eierspätzle (egg spätzle), Schweinebraten (roast pork), Wiener Schnitzel or Apfelstrudel you can't go wrong with Weltrestaurant Markthalle (*Pücklerstr. 34, Friedrichshain-Kreuzberg, 10997*). When you need an easy afternoon, make yourself comfortable with a crafted coffee brewed in any number of the specialty cafés. Berliners care about coffee, and know precisely how it needs to be made. The same philosophy goes into their homemade pastries, cakes and pies. So, sit back and tuck in!

# 60X60 : RESTAURANTS & CAFÉS

**Aram Bartholl**
*Artist*

I like to make art about Internet and computers. It is great to be based in cozy Berlin while travelling worldwide to shows, workshops or talks.

## Companion Coffee
P.071

**Kristín Björk Kristjánsdóttir**, *Composer*

I am a composer and visual artist, also known as Kira Kira, making adventurous electronic music and film. I moved to Berlin from Iceland about five years ago.

**Julio Rölle**
*Designer, 44flavours*

I'm Julio Rölle, a German artist with French and Belgian roots. With my friend Sebastian Bagge we run the art and design collective 44flavours.

## Mörder
P.070

## Kaffeeladen Görlitzer Bahnhof
P.072

**Stahl R**
*Graphic design studio*

Stahl R was founded in 2012 by Tobias Röttger and Susanne Stahl. We create unique design solutions for a broad range of clients from both commercial and cultural fields.

## Five Elephant
P.074

**Anna Rose**
*Photographer*

As a third generation "Berliner," I love the city like no other. I work as a photographer shooting for various German and international magazines.

**Danae Diaz**
*Illustrator & animation artist*

I'm from Spain and I came here about ten years ago to finish my Fine Art degree, then I fell in love with the city. Since then I have been living in the areas of Kreuzberg and Neukölln.

## Gipfeltreffen
P.073

## Café Atlantic
P.075

**Timm Kekeritz**
*Founder, Raureif*

I'm an interaction designer, software expert and simplicity enthusiast from Berlin, and creators of iOS apps Partly Cloudy, EcoChallenge, and Virtual Water.

Café Lois
P.077

**Oliver Moore**
*Co-founder, SSAWSTUDIO*

I'm a graphic designer, art director, founder of multi-brand store SSAW Store and co-founder of SSAWSTUDIO a multidisciplinary graphic design and communication studio.

**Eps51**
*Graphic design studio*

We actively develop visual concepts with a strong focus on typography and bilingual design. Most of our clients are from the fields of arts and culture, fashion and design.

Kochu Karu
P.076

Lavanderia Vecchia
P.078

**Rilla Alexander**
*Designer & illustrator*

I am an Australian designer and illustrator who has lived in Berlin for eight years. I live life hand in hand with my alter-ego Sozi who features in my first picture book "Her Idea."

Kimchi Princess
P.081

**Fons Hickmann**
*Founder, Fons Hickmann m23*

I'm a graphic designer, writer and founder of Berlin-based design studio, Fons Hickmann m23. I'm also a professor at Berlin University of the Arts.

**Nadine Goepfert**
*Textile designer*

My work is based on research and conceptual thinking and explores the wide field of eventualities by creating open situations, with an interest in craftsmanship and traditional textile techniques.

Clärchens Ballhaus
P.080

Da Baffi
P.082

### Mörder
Map E, P.105

With postcards and pamphlets stuck all over the door, found furniture and celadon walls, the charismatic setting of this neatly equipped café might not evoke what its name "Murder" denotes, but the friendly staff here are definitely capable of making killer coffee, toasts and sandwiches at prices to die for. A bonus to their specialty menu is an array of exceptional snacks available at the counter and made in-house daily. Ask for a macchiato latte and while away your afternoon roadside or in the backyard. If you're lucky, there might be a mini-art show going on.

- 0830-1800 (M-F)
- Torstr. 199 (Entrance on Borsigstr.), Mitte, 10115
- +49 (0)30 26 37 11 55
- unternehmen-mitte.de

*"Best coffee place in Mitte. Be nice to Tönjes! He is my most important adviser!"*
– Aram Bartholl

### 38 Companion Coffee
*Map A, P.102*

The young founders and baristas of Companion Coffee, Chris Onton and Shawn Barber, know their stuff and brew top-rated coffee. Sharing a courtyard with VooStore (#25), this cozy café serves specialty coffee and tea six days a week accompanied by a choice of baked goods, and sells designer furniture created and manufactured by Sigurd Larsen, one of the contributors to this guide. The café also stocks grinders, filters and freshly roasted coffee by premium coffee specialists including Johannes Bayer and Five Elephant (#41) to take home.

- 1100-1900 (M-Sa)
- Oranienstr. 24, Kreuzberg, 10999
- +49 (0)17 66 34 46 225
- www.companioncoffee.com

> "They have the most delicious coffee in Berlin. I feel lucky that this grand establishment is right across the street from my studio. It's my 'Cheers,' if you will."
>
> – Kristin Björk Kristjansdottir, Kira Kira

###  Kaffeeladen Görlitzer Bahnhof
*Map A, P.102*

Life-size paintings and a beautiful poster collection forms just a small part of this café's free spirit vibe. The fresh bakery produces homemade focaccia, ciabatta, cakes and cookies and adds to the homespun charm. Coffee is made using directly traded coffee, sourced from Ecuador, Brazil and Guatemala, and roasted and brewed on site. Hearty fresh sandwiches are an ideal accompaniment to your daily fix.

- 0730–1800 (M-F), 0900– (Sa), 1000–1600 (Su)
- Manteuffelstr. 87, Kreuzberg, 10997
- +49 (0)30 69 54 99 28
- www.goerlitzerbahnhof.de

*"The owners Jo and Ramin are good people. If the weather is great you can sit in front of the store and observe everyday neighbourhood life. Great spot!"*
– Julio Rölle, 44flavours

## 40 Gipfeltreffen
Map A, P.102

The name of this place translates as 'a meeting at the mountain top,' and that's exactly how it feels here. With wooden flooring, white walls and sturdy old furniture, the café exudes peace and quiet that helps leave the outside hustle of Kreuzberg behind. Opening early and closing late, this place produces nourishing breakfasts and short but enticing lunch and dinner menus, all at very fair prices. Go here to unfreeze in winter as the log fireplace spreads a rosy, warm glow.

- 0900–0000 (M–F), 1000– (Sa–Su)
- Görlitzer Str. 68, Kreuzberg, 10997
- +49 (0)30 68 07 70 11
- gipfeltreffen-kreuzberg.de

"*Have breakfast on a Saturday or Sunday. They take no reservations, so be there right when it opens.*"
– Stahl R

60X60 : RESTAURANTS & CAFÉS

### 41 Five Elephant
*Map L, P.109*

Five Elephant has two standouts: freshly-roasted specialty coffee and Philadelphia cheesecake, made by passionate owners Kris Schackman and Sophie Weigensamer. Tucked away in the treelined residential stretch of Reichenberger Straße in Kreuzberg, this independent roaster-café produces some of the city's best roasts and brews with a Diedrich roasting machine and directly traded beans. Should trying the coffee at Five Elephant leave you with a permanent hankering, their beans can be shipped worldwide.

- 0830-1900 (M-F), 1000- (Sa-Su)
- Reichenberger Str. 101, Kreuzberg, 10999
- www.fiveelephant.com

*"Get the cheesecake!"*
– Anna Rose

### 42 Café Atlantic
Map H, P.107

Traditional German brekkie is a promise of fulfilment. Give it a try at Café Atlantic and ask for *Frühstück für Zwei* (breakfast for two). Soon you'll have plates brimming with German breads, honey, jams, nutella, sausages, cold-cuts, cheese, quark cheese, boiled eggs, breakfast cereal, yogurt, juice, fruit and vegetables to fuel your body and soul. Besides wide-reaching German breakfasts, multinational breakfast options like English, Norwegian, Italian, Swiss, American, French and Danish, as well as vegetarian, are served until 5pm. Grab a seat outdoors to enjoy your food while observing the happy neighbourhood vibe.

- 0900–0200 daily
- Bergmannstr. 100, Kreuzberg, 10961
- +49 (0)30 69 19 292

*"'Frühstück für Zwei' is amazing!"*
— Danae Diaz

60X60 : **RESTAURANTS & CAFÉS**

### 43 Kochu Karu
*Map E, P.105*

This Korean-Spanish restaurant dabbles with the essence of both cuisines. Managed by co-owners and chefs, Spanish José Miranda Morillo and Korean Bini Lee-Zauner, the kitchen creates inspirational appetisers combining the concept of tapas with *banchan* (Korean side dishes) using fresh organic ingredients. Imagine calamari salad with chorizo sausage in Korean hot pepper sauce and bibimbap in Korean tacos, with grilled tomatoes and guacamole on the side. Kochu Karu also hosts the much-touted "sing-meal" every month, where Morillo will remain behind the kitchen and Lee-Zauner focuses on her songs.

- 🕐 1200-2230 (Tu-F), 1400- (Sa-Su & P.H.)
- 🏠 Eberswalder Str. 35, Prenzlauer Berg, 10437
- ☎ +49 (0)30 80 93 81 91   URL www.kochukaru.de

"*Every first Thursday evening of each month, the 4-course 'Singmahl' elevates the great fusion cuisine with the chansons of the chef herself.*"
– Timm Kekeritz, Raureif

## 44 Café Lois
Map E, P.105

At a quiet corner off the hip and noisy Torstraße, Lois serves one of the town's best coffee, pastries and homemade quiches by day and then transforms into a friendly cocktail bar by night. A highlight is their daily soup, created from seasonal flavours that are sure to boost your mood. It can be particularly difficult to snag a seat outdoors on a sunny day, but the scenic beauty lasts till dusk, and the evening twilight here is unforgettable. Order an aperitif and pair it with a bowl of salted almonds, hand-roasted from the owner's family recipe.

- 0800-0000 (M-F), 0900- (Sa-Su)
- Linienstr. 60, Mitte, 10119
- +49 (0)17 97 04 90 41
- CafeLois

*"With a laid back atmosphere, this is one of the rare spots in Mitte where the sun can be enjoyed from early morning till sunset."*

– Oliver Moore, SSAWSTUDIO

 **Lavanderia Vecchia**
Map L, P.109

Relish the taste of Italian home cooking from the Sabine region. Called "Old Laundry" – after what the premises were formerly used for, Lavanderia Vecchia expertly prepares classic dishes that make use of the best oils and fresh ingredients. Enjoy soups, pastas, fish and Italian desserts from the à la carte lunch menu in the restaurant's delightful backyard, or sample their degustation dinner menu for a fulfilling evening. At €58 per person, you will have antipasti (with up to ten varieties), primi, secondi, and dolci courses and half a litre of wine all to yourself. Arrive at 7.30pm on the day and wait to be served.

- 1200-1430 (Tu-F), 1930-2300 (Tu-Sa)
- 2F Hof Fabrikgebäude EG, Flughafenstr. 46, Neukölln, 12053
- +49 (0)30 62 72 21 52
- www.lavanderiavecchia.de
- Dinner by appointment only

*"Super relaxed atmosphere, friendly staff and amazing Italian cuisine. Reserve a table in advance!"*
– Eps51

60X60 : **RESTAURANTS & CAFÉS**

### 46  Clärchens Ballhaus

Map E, P.105

Clärchens Ballhaus has been celebrating high spirits in its restaurant and ballroom for over 100 years. Here you can have delicious food at long tables alongside crowds of jubilant dancers who Vogue one minute and then seamlessly segue into Salsa the next. Before joining the dancers, fuel up with yummy pizza, *schnitzel* (fried pork with breadcrumb coating) and *kartoffel* (potato) salad. Also peek into the *Spiegelsaal* (Hall of Mirrors) on the first floor, which is still in its original condition and functions as a chamber music performance venue. The eyecatching advertising poster is an original painted by Otto Dix (1891-1969).

- 🕐 *1100 till late daily*
- 🏠 *Auguststr. 24, Mitte, 10117*
- 📞 *+49 (0)30 28 29 295*
- 🌐 *www.ballhaus.de, www.spiegelsaal-berlin.de*

"*Clärchens Ballhaus feels like pure Berlin to me. It's a rare restaurant in Berlin that accepts credit cards and splitting the bill is normal here.*"
– Rilla Alexander

## 47 Kimchi Princess
*Map A, P.102*

Sitting at heart of hipster district Kreuzberg, Kimchi Princess is committed to taking authentic Korean dining in Berlin to a new level. Starting out as a small pop-up eatery at the Berlin Design Market, followed by opening Soju Bar and Angry Chicken, the Korean kitchen is now a fully-fledged restaurant with comfortable seating and communal tables. Diners smack their lips over winning kimchi, spicy chicken and other delicious classics like bibimbap, barbeque grills, snacks and a vegetarian range. Kimchi Princess gets packed quickly, so if you forget to book a table, try a takeaway.

- 1200-2300 daily
- Skalizer Str. 36, Kreuzberg, 10999 (entrance on Manteuffelstr.)
- +49 (0)16 34 58 02 03
- www.kimchiprincess.com

"A stylish-asia-scene-restaurant with stylish-asia-scene-food. Just enjoy sitting outside having a drink and some spicy food."

– Fons Hickmann, Fons Hickmann m23

60X60 : **RESTAURANTS & CAFÉS**

 **Da Baffi**
*Map I, P.108*

This simple, stylish Italian kitchen eschews all things fancy to focus on authentic Bologna-inspired dishes and celebrates the roots of two co-owners. The inclusion of regional specialties like parmesan cheese and parma ham, although expected, still constitute a surprise when matched with a handpicked wine list and German produce. A four-course menu often begins with freshly-baked bread and a mixed starter, followed by homemade pasta or risotto. For secondi, it is highly-recommended to order seafood, as their chef has clearly mastered his craft.

- 1830 till late (Tu-Sa)
- Nazarethkirchstr. 41, Wedding, 13347
- +49 (0)17 56 92 65 45
- www.dabaffi.com
- Cash only

"Here you don't get any over-decorated plates, but delicious authentic Italian cuisine and great wines."

– Nadine Goepfert

# Nightlife

Wild parties, eclectic music and premium German beers

"Nightlife" sounds too narrow a word to describe what's offered after dark in Berlin. If you wish to party like a Berliner, you could be revelling from dusk till noon, and throughout the weekend. Notable as one of the world's greatest music capitals and cradle of European Techno music, Berlin certainly throbs with electric beats. Party in Berlin is wild and primitive and who knows what could happen in smoky-sordid basements or equally at world-famous clubs like Berghain (#49). Life for non-party goers is also diverse and exciting – try watching a concert staged in a drained swimming pool (#60) for starters. If you just want to chill, characterful bars are aplenty; try pub crawling on Weserstraße, or pop into posh cocktail lounges (#54), jazz bars (#52) and micro breweries with premium German beer (#50) on your doorstep. Another common Berliner pastime is to hang out in front of a "Späti," little stores that open 24-7, selling almost everything from drinks to small electronic toys. After clubbing, grab a beer (try cheaper-than-water Sternburg, or "Sterni") or Club Mate (X'mas edition) at one of the many in Friedrichshain, sit on the railroad bridge Modersohnbrücke and delight as guitar players strum and watch the sunrise.

## 60X60 : NIGHTLIFE

**Sebastian Haslauer**
*Artist & illustrator*

I publish art books and fanzines and host a music show on arte. I made money by selling beard growth remedy to Berlin newbies but lost all of it on the racecourse. I can play diabolo.

# Hops & Barley
P.089

**Michael Wickert**
*Smokemaster, GLUT & SPÄNE*

I bring a new twist to the traditional preservation method of smoking and create mouthwatering fish delicacies at GLUT & SPÄNE, Berlin's first sustainable fish smokery in Markthalle Neun.

**Sera Yong**
*Illustrator & graphic designer*

My name is Sera Yong, based in both Berlin and Seoul. I am currently working at design studio HORT and also doing some freelance work with nice people from all over the world.

# Berghain / Panorama Bar
P.088

# Salon zur Wilden Renate
P.090

**Patricia Waller**
*Artist*

In a subversive tongue-in-cheek manner, I mix together the absurd and the bizarre, to create my work, and all I need is a crochet hook.

# Jungbusch Berlin
P.093

**Jose Romussi Murphy**
*Artist*

I am Jose Romussi, an autodidact artist from Chile. After many trips around the world, I decided to live in Berlin. I've been working in my studio for a year and a half.

**Jürgen Mayer H.**
*Founder, J. MAYER H.*

I'm the founder and principal of cross-disciplinary studio J. MAYER H. in Berlin. My work is part of numerous collections including MoMA and SFMOMA.

# Yorck-schlösschen
P.092

# Bar Tausend
P.094

**Jens Lausenmeyer**
*Art director, boymeetsgirl design*

I'm a passionate Berlin-based design and art director, loving good (vegan) food, gin and electronical music.

**Georgia Hill**
*Typographer & illustrator*

I'm a freelance custom typographer and illustrator from Sydney, Australia, who has lived in Berlin for a year.

**Luciano Foglia**
*Visual artist*

I have been working in interactive design, art and music since 2001. I work commercially as senior interactive designer and art director.

**Joy Wellboy**
*Music duo*

We are Joy Wellboy, a duo from Brussels currently living in Berlin. We make music, videos and photos.

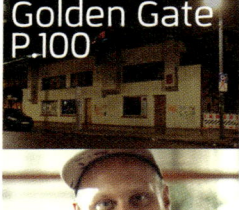

**Stephan Hartmann**
*CEO & creative director, 908*

38, family guy, married with two lovely kids. I have a weakness for red wine, dead French writers and TV series but not in that exact order.

**Robert G. Bartholot**
*Visual artist*

My name is Robert G. Bartholot and I am a Berlin-based visual artist focusing on photographic illustration.

## NIGHTLIFE

### 49 Berghain / Panorama Bar
*Map A, P.102*

Comprised of four parts – Berghain, the main room; Panorama Bar, the impeccably clean and organised upstair bar; Lab.Oratory, the men-only club on 1F and Berghain Kantine the adjacent smaller club, this giant club remains a huge draw for techno lovers. The architecture and sheer scale of a power plant, as well as its eclectic music mix always call up a huge queue every weekend. The door policy, however, is pretty strict (and random), especially for tourists. Dress up, avoid big groups, keep a low profile and be polite to increase your chance of getting in.

🕐 Opening hours vary with programmes 🏠 Am Wriezener Bahnhof, Friedrichshain, 10243
📞 +49 (0)30 29 36 02 10
🌐 www.berghain.de
📎 18+, Cash only

*"It is not about seeing and being seen, about chatting and blasphemy, drinking or flirting. Berghain is about dancing, drugs, euphoria, sex and oblivion."*
– Sebastian Haslauer

## 50 Hops & Barley
Map A, P.103

No trip to Berlin is complete without German beer. Local bar and microbrewery Hops & Barley is the place for decent craft beers and cider freshly poured from casks. Their pilsner is highly sought-after, with a menu rounded out with dark and wheat beers as well as featured beer specials, expertly matched with grainy breads, bar snacks and a warm neighbourhood vibe. Want to drink free of worries? Book one of two guest rooms for €28 per person and visit East Side Gallery the next morning, which is just 20-minute walk away.

- 1700 till late daily
- Wühlischstr. 22/23, Friedrichshain, 10245
- +49 (0)30 29 36 75 34
- www.hopsandbarley-berlin.de

*"Accompany your beer and bread with Schmalzstulle (spicy lard) and a football match on the screen. This is the perfect start to a Berlin night!"*
– Michael Wickert, GLUT & SPÄNE

# NIGHTLIFE

### 51 Salon zur Wilden Renate
Map A, P.103

Truly an otherworldly club, Salon zur Wilden Renate is set inside a decadent two-storey mansion in East Berlin. The club dares you to take a trip down to its labyrinth – a wild art installation put up by two German artists – or dance on someone else's bed. Flashy-trashy dance parties happen all year round across three dance floors that appear a little different every night. In summer, Uncle Tom's Cabin, in the courtyard, serves up techno and electric music.

- 1800-0000 (W-Sa)   €10 coverage
- Alt-Stralau 70, Friedrichshain, 10245
- +49 (0)30 25 04 14 26   www.renate.cc
- Walk-ins only

"All music genres are happening in different WG rooms all at once. It makes me feel I am at someone's house party. A cute garden adds charm to everything else."
– Sera Yong

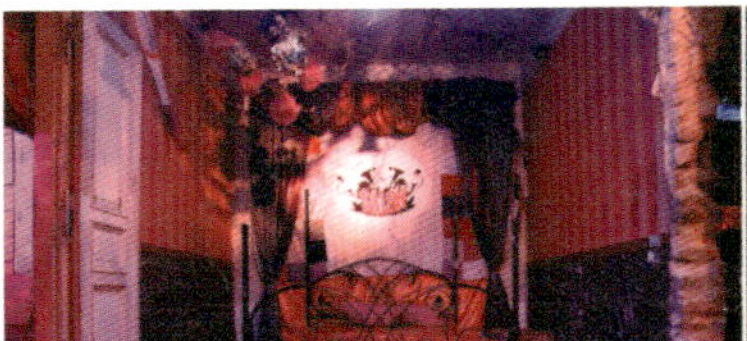

## 52 Yorckschlösschen
Map H, P.107

Having stood in Kreuzberg for more than a century, Yorckschlösschen is a legendary jazz club that entertains all. Traditional jazz, blues, swing, funk, soul and R&B rings through a tavern-style interior and, in summer, a charming beer garden. On their menu, you will find central European dishes and Sunday brunch at friendly prices. Live jazz sessions come on Thursdays and Fridays in winter-time, or Wednesdays and weekends at other times of the year, for €4–8 per head.

- 1700–0300 (M–Sa), 1000–0200 (Su)
- Yorckstr. 15, Kreuzberg, 10965
- www.yorckschloesschen.de

*"You can hear the best in New Orleans jazz, soul and blues here."*
– Patricia Waller

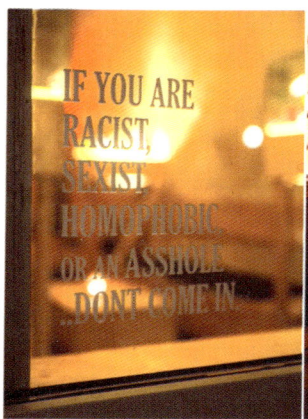

###  Jungbusch Berlin
Map L, P.109

Jungbusch offers more than just cocktails. Run by two fun-loving young men, and installed with self-made box-shaped furniture throughout, the bar doubles as an exhibition space for illustrations, photography, installation, music performance and the owners' favourite toy figures! Opened in spring 2013, the bar has quickly grown into a creative den at the heart of Neukölln. Original door signage at the bar proclaims they welcome no racists, sexists, homophobics or assholes...

- 1900 till late daily (except Su in winter)
- Weserstr. 16, Neukölln, 12047
- jungbuschberlin.de

*"Nice people, easy style, good music, not to hip."*
– Jose Romussi Murphy

60X60 : **NIGHTLIFE**

### 54 Bar Tausend
Map E, P.104

Down under the rail bridge near Friedrichstraße station, an unmarked iron door leads revellers to a lively, futuristic cocktail bar with a touch of the 1920s. Glammed up with glass and steel decor, this chic club is not only illuminated by gigantic donut-shaped lighting but also a sophisticated crowd often composed of film-makers, architects and the young fashionable set. Listen to the ambient house, funk, blues and jazz live from 10pm. Bar Tausend also houses a bar serving inspired Asian and Spanish-influenced American food.

- 1930 till late (Tu-Sa)
- Schiffbauerdamm 11, Mitte, 10117
- +49 (0)30 27 58 20 70
- www.tausendberlin.com
- 18+

"*A cool and stylish place with the best cocktails you can get in Berlin-Mitte. Always very crowded.*"
– Jürgen Mayer H., J. MAYER H.

094

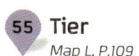 **Tier**
Map L, P.109

Standing in the pub-filled Weserstraße, Tier catches the posh, grown-up crowd's eyes with their Nighthawks-esque ambience and specialty drinks. Homemade syrup is just one of the magic tricks that Tier's cocktail pundits do. Since 2012, this corner-bar has surprised regulars and pleased whiskey nuts and gin addicts literally every week by bringing new twists and seasonal sensations into old classics. Tier admits groups of no more than six.

- 1900–0200 daily
- Weserstr. 42, Neukölln, 12045
- TiERBAR
- 18+, Cash only

> "Location is very nice with a good choice of different gins. Hip and young. Don't go before 12pm."
>
> – Jens Lausenmeyer, boymeetsgirl design

## 56 Michelberger Hotel

Map A, P.102

More than just a hip hotel for budget travellers, Michelberger Hotel is a happy creative family eager to provide a home from home, with everything cool and quirky – from interior decorations to drink menu and schnapps bottles – all created in-house. Walk through a giant monkey mouth, before you know it it'll be 4am and the schnapps will still be flowing in the cosy Honolulu bar. Revel in house-party sets in the courtyard during summer and stay warm with mulled wine and live shows in the beautiful lobby in winter. As they say, they are always open!

- Warschauer Str. 39/40, Friedrichshain, 10243
- +49 (0)30 29 77 85 90
- www.michelbergerhotel.com

*"Having worked here for a year, I'm a little bit biased... but it's a clear sign of how much I love the place."*
– Georgia Hill

60X60 : NIGHTLIFE

### 57 Kuschlowski
Map L, P.109

Managed by furniture designer and co-owner Daniel Neugebauer, the retro interior features colourful, handcrafted furniture for a happy neighbourhood vibe. Among the many nice little pubs on Weserstraße, Kuschlowski stands out with its excellent vodka selection made up from largely Russian, Polish and Ukrainian brands. Crowds convene at the front of the door in summertime and around an open fire in winter. A stack of complementary pretzel sticks ultimately seals the deal.

- 2000 till late daily
- Weserstr. 202, Neukölln, 12047
- +49 (0)17 62 43 89 701
- www.kuschlowski.de

*"Ask the friendly staff to assist you in finding the right vodka. If you don't fancy vodka they also serve bottled beer."*

– Luciano Foglia

### 58 Slaughterhouse
*Map E, P.104*

The biggest attraction of this underground Berliner club is the extensive list of music genres played. Indie, punk, ska, goth rock, 80s/90s wave and even Turkish pop can all be found loud on the speakers. An advocate of new music, expect wild parties and concerts hosted by rated DJs and budding musicians and bands. Past appearances include Schlechte Liebhaber and Isolation Berlin. Find Slaughterhouse in the backyard of cooperative complex Kulturfabrik Moabit. Take the S-bahn to Wedding then bus M27 to Quitzowstraße.

🕒 *2300-0600 (F-Sa)*
🏠 *Kulturfabrik, Lehrter Str. 35, Moabit, 10557*
🔗 *www.slaughterhouse-berlin.de*

*"Go observe new wave tracks or look at people moving to the underground sounds of the 1980s in the dark. They are really exaggerated with the smoke-machine also!"*

– Joy Wellboy

 **Golden Gate**
Map A, P.102

Dirty, weird, ecstatic, voluptuous, wacky, bonkers, cranky, loco and bananas – that is how Afterhour at Golden Gate is described. Nestled in a graffiti-wrapped brick house underneath the rails close to Jannowitzbrücke station, the seedy joint collides the chatter of trains, with up-front tech house all night long spun by top-notch Berlin-based DJs. Marathon parties start on Thursday nights and finish on Friday afternoon, followed by Afterhour on Saturday that doesn't kick out until sunrise Monday.

- 2300 till late (Th–Su)
- Schicklerstr. 4, Mitte, 10179
- +49 (0)30 57 70 42 78
- www.goldengate-berlin.de
- Cash only

"*Afterhour at Golden Gate is a close encounter of the third kind. If you're not posh and spoiled then it's a good spot to grab the last 2 or 5 beers before you faint.*"

– Stephan Hartmann, 908

## 60 Stadtbad Wedding
*Map I, P.108*

If you've already partied Berlin-style on rooftops and defunct factories, perhaps it's time to gather in and around a drained swimming pool while watching an orchestra or a theatrical work playing down at the other end. Highlights here have included underground music shows by Boiler Room's outpost in Berlin. Stadtbad Wedding (also Stattbad) is a former bathhouse drawn up by Berliner architect Ludwig Hoffmann (1852-1932) before being rebuilt into a municipal pool after WWII. Its latest incarnation is a hotspot for exhibitions, concerts, filmmaking and screenprint festival, Druck Berlin.

Opening hours vary with events
Gerichtstr. 65, Gesundbrunnen, 13347
URL www.stattbad.net

*"Check the calendar for their programmes or just have lunch or a coffee in Stattbar. The appendant garden hits the Panke, a hidden canal with trails to stroll up."*

– Robert G. Bartholot

DISTRICT MAP : **FRIEDRICHSHAIN, KREUZBERG, MITTE**

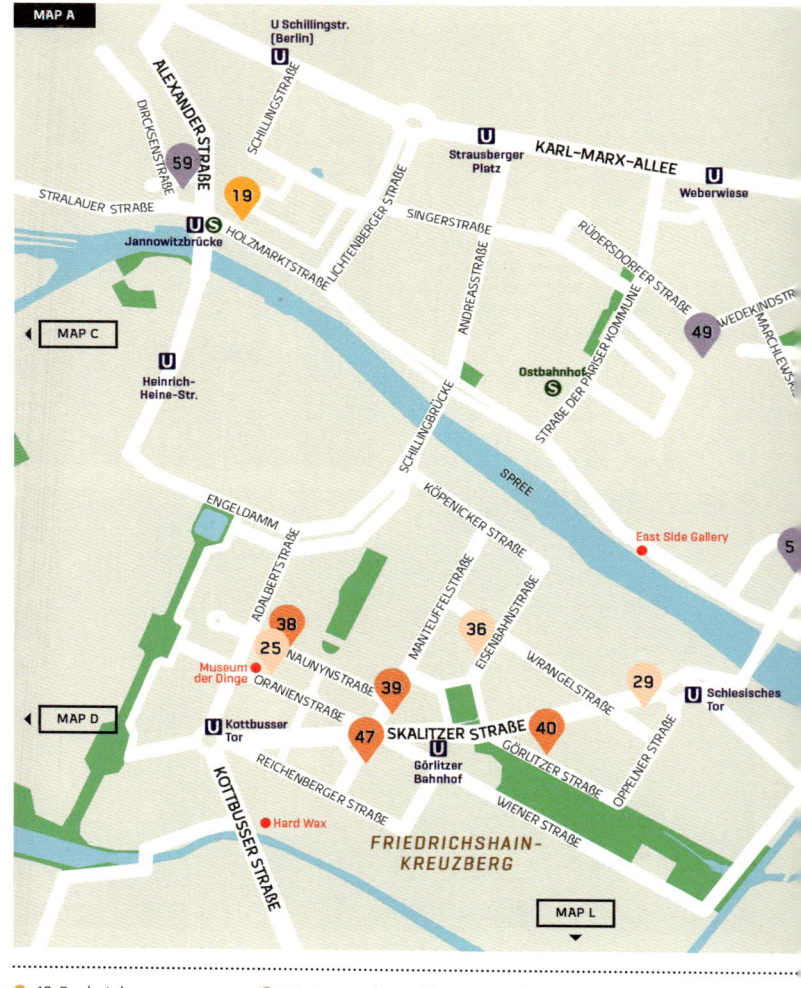

- 19_Buchstabenmuseum
- 25_VooStore
- 29_Motto Berlin
- 36_Markthalle Neun
- 38_Companion Coffee
- 39_Kaffeeladen Görlitzer Bahnhof
- 40_Gipfeltreffen
- 47_Kimchi Princess
- 49_Berghain / Panorama Bar
- 56_Michelberger Hotel
- 59_Golden Gate

DISTRICT MAPS : **PRENZLAUER BERG, MITTE, KREUZBERG**

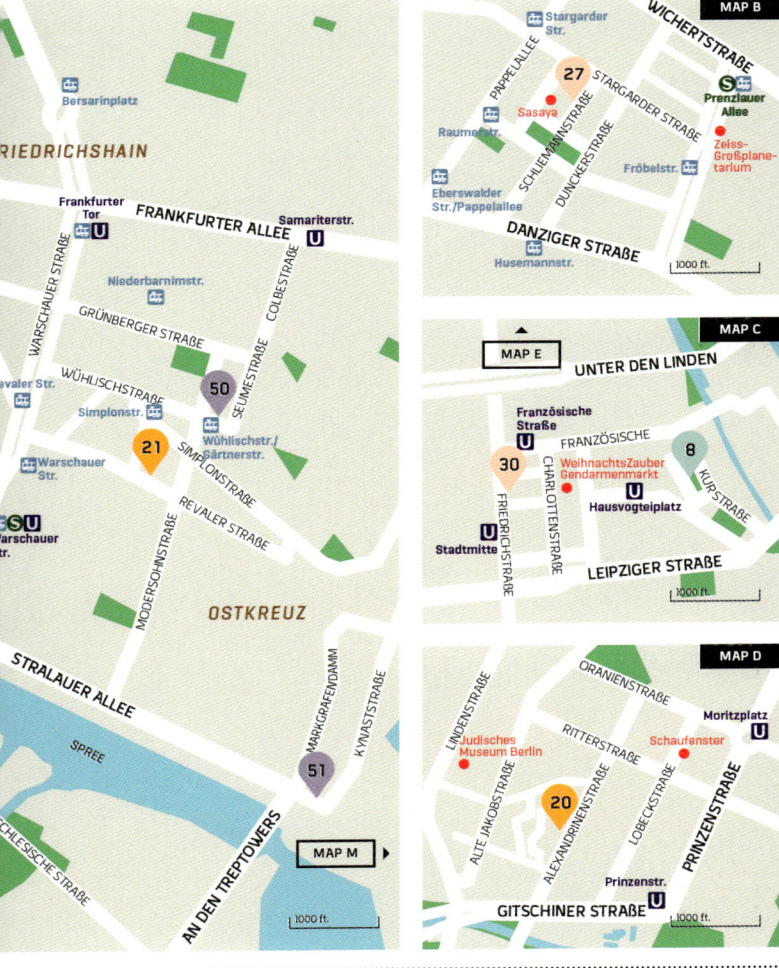

- 8_Caroline-von-Humboldt-Weg
- 20_ST. AGNES
- 21_Revaler Straße
- 27_RAUM Italic (SPAZIO Corsivo)
- 30_Quartier 206
- 50_Hops & Barley
- 51_Salon zur Wilden Renate

DISTRICT MAP : **MOABIT, MITTE, PRENZLAUER BERG, MUSEUMSINSEL**

- 4_Deutsches Historisches Museum
- 13_Neues Museum
- 14_Bode-Museum
- 16_Platoon Kunsthalle Berlin
- 17_Kunstwerke Berlin
- 22_Sammlung Boros
- 23_Ehemalige Jüdische Mädchenschule
- 32_Dudes Factory
- 34_Trödelmarkt Arkonaplatz

- 37_Mörder
- 43_Kochu Karu
- 44_Café Lois
- 46_Clärchens Ballhaus
- 54_Bar Tausend
- 58_Slaughterhouse

DISTRICT MAP : **FRIEDRICHSHAGEN**

● 35_Flohmarkt Friedrichshagen

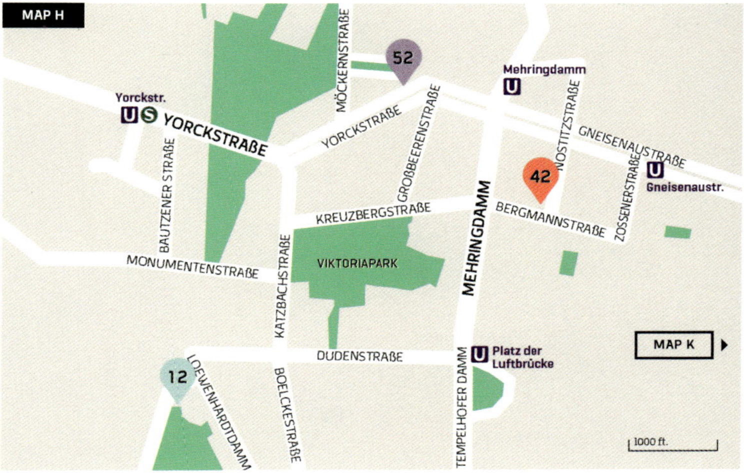

DISTRICT MAPS: **TIERGARTEN, KREUZBERG, TEMPELHOF**

## MAP G

## MAP H

- 3_Bauhaus-Archiv
- 9_Shell-Haus
- 12_Schwerbelastungskörper
- 15_Martin-Gropius-Bau
- 24_Galerie Thomas Fischer
- 26_Andreas Murkudis
- 42_Café Atlantic
- 52_Yorckschlösschen

DISTRICT MAPS : WEDDING, GESUNDBRUNNEN, CHARLOTTENBURG, TEMPELHOF

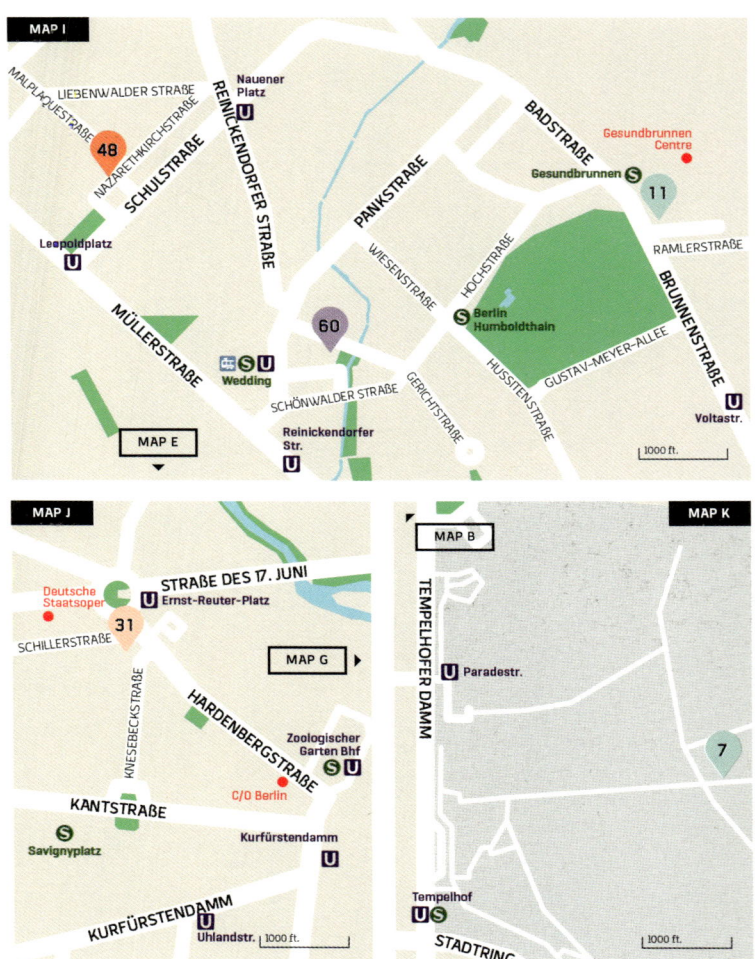

- 7_Tempelhofer Freiheit
- 11_Berliner Unterwelten
- 31_Manufactum
- 48_Da Baffi
- 60_Stadtbad Wedding

DISTRICT MAP : **KREUZBERG, NEUKÖLLN**

- 28_Süper Store
- 33_Nowkölln Flowmarkt
- 41_Five Elephant
- 45_Lavanderia Vecchia
- 53_Jungbusch Berlin
- 55_Tier
- 57_Kuschlowski

DISTRICT MAP : **ALT-TREPTOW, PLÄNTERWALD**

- 1_Sowjetisches Ehrenmal
- 2_Spreepark
- 51_Salon zur Wilden Renate

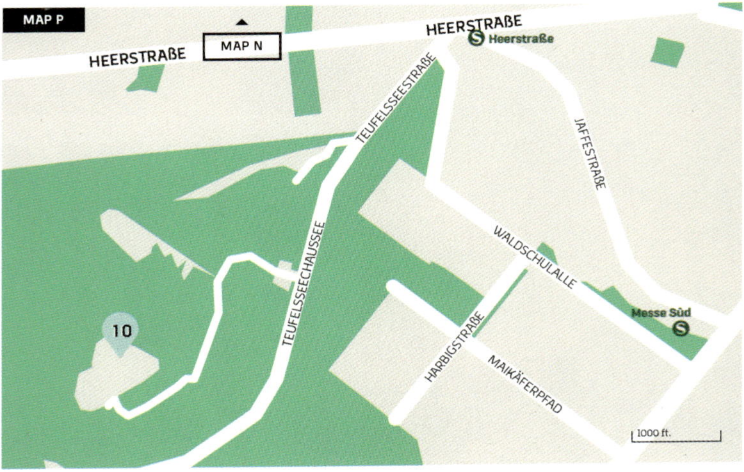

DISTRICT MAPS : **WESTEND, NEUKÖLLN, GRUNEWALD**

- 5_Corbusierhaus
- 6_Gropiusstadt
- 10_Teufelsberg

# Accommodations

Hip hostels, fully-equipped apartments & swanky hotels

No journey is perfect without a good night's sleep to recharge. Whether you're backpacking or on a business trip, our picks combine top quality and convenience, whatever your budget.

**⑤** < €80  **⑤** €81–200  **⑤** €201+

## Hüttenpalast

Rooms at Hüttenpalast are a caravan or wooden hut within a converted vacuum-cleaner factory, offering an indoors camping party inside the city. Should the modern take on caravanning not appeal, six standard rooms are available, and are, unlike the camping area, ensuite. Café serves mainly vegetarian and organic staples and sits next to a beautiful garden rich with flora and herbs.

🏠 Hobrechtstr. 65/66, Neukölln, 12047
☎ +49 (0)30 37 30 58 06
🔗 www.huettenpalast.de

## Tautes Heim

Design history lovers get a one-off experience at the carefully restored end-terrace house once a part of iconic architect Bruno Taut's historic "horseshoe" estate. Original fittings, flooring and tiled stoves remain, with a studious update faithful to the Bauhaus modernist design.

*Neukölln-Britz, 12359*
*+49 (0)30 60 10 71 93*
*www.tautes-heim.de*

## Modern Houseboat

It's possible to enjoy tranquility and isolation in central Berlin. With a generous living area, open plan kitchen, bathroom, double bedroom, central heating and fireplace, this floating house set on Lake Rummelsburg is no different to any grounded modern home. Public transit and hip diners are just a stone's throw away.

🏠 *Gustav-Holzmann-Str. 10, Lichtenberg, 10317* URL *Bookings: welcomebeyond.com*

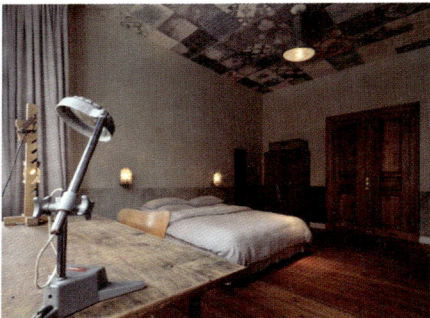

### Linnen
🏠 Eberswalder str. 35, Prenzlauer Berg, 10437  ☎ +49 (0)30 47 37 24 40
🔗 www.linnenberlin.com

### Casa Camper Berlin
🏠 Weinmeisterstr. 1, Mitte, 10178
☎ +49 (0)30 20 00 34 10
🔗 www.casacamper.com

### Generator Hostel (Mitte)
🏠 Oranienburger Str. 65, Mitte, 10117
☎ +49 (0)30 92 10 37 680
🔗 generatorhostels.com

ACCOMMODATIONS

### Gorki Apartments

🏠 Weinbergsweg 25, Mitte, 10119
☎ +49 (0)30 48 49 64 80
URL www.gorkiapartments.de

### Miniloft

🏠 Hessische str. 5, Mitte, 10115
☎ +49 (0)30 84 71 090
URL www.miniloft.com

### Plus One Berlin
### The Apartment

🏠 Reuterstr. 28, Neukölln, 12047
☎ +49 (0)17 83 59 35 17
URL www.plusoneberlin.com

# Notes

# Index

## Architecture

**Jürgen Mayer H.
@J. MAYER H.**, p094
www.jmayerh.de
Portrait by Paul Green

**Sigurd Larsen**, p052
www.sigurdlarsen.eu

## Art & Illustration

**Aram Bartholl**, p070
www.datenform.de
Portrait by Eva Paulsen

**Danae Diaz**, p075
www.danaediaz.com

**Eyal Burstein**, p022
www.eyalburstein.com

**Jeongmoon Choi**, p034
www.jeongmoon.de

**Jose Romussi Murphy**, p093
cargocollective.com/joseromussi

**Judith Seng**, p056
www.judithseng.de
Portrait by Steven James Scott

**Lisa Rienermann**, p020
lisarienermann.com

**Patricia Waller**, p092
www.patriciawaller.com

**Sebastian Haslauer**, p088
www.hasimachtsachen.com

## Branding & Advertising

**Jens Lausenmeyer
@boymeetsgirl design**, p095
www.boymeetsgirl.de

**Li Wolfgang Schiffer**, p042
(Agency) www.n-o-agency.com
(Sales representatives)
www.celluloid-vfx.com
www.woodblock.tv

**Raban Ruddigkeit
@+ Ruddigkeit**, p036
www.ruddigkeit.de
Portrait by Valentino Griscioli

## Fashion

**Martin Niklas Wieser**, p016
www.martinniklaswieser.com
Portrait by Daryl Natale

**Michael Sontag**, p058
www.michaelsontag.com
Portrait by Christian Schwarzenberg

**Nadine Goepfert**, p082
www.nadinegoepfert.com
Portrait by Patrick Desbrosses

**Potipoti**, p040
www.potipoti.com
Portrait by Chus Antón

**Sissi Goetze**, p032
www.sissigoetze.com
Portrait by Andreas Muehe

**Veronika Wildgruber**, p065
www.veronikawildgruber.com

## Film

**Ben & Julia**, p043
www.benandjulia.com

## Food

**Michael Wickert
@GLUT & SPÄNE**, p089
www.glutundspaene.de

**Nicky&Max**, p046
nickyandmax.com

**Our/Berlin**, p044
www.ourberlin.de
www.paulsanders.de

**Pret A Diner**, p017
www.koflerkompanie.com,
www.oliviasteele.com
www.pretadiner.com
Portrait by Georg Roske

## Graphics

**Azar Kazimir
@Michelberger Hotel**, p014
www.michelbergerhotel.com

**Enrico Bonafede @Mjölk**, p018
www.studiomjolk.com

**Eps51**, p078
www.eps51.com

**Fons Hickmann
@Fons Hickmann m23**, p081
www.m23.de

**Georgia Hill**, p096
georgiahill.tumblr.com

**Guillaume Kashima**, p060
www.behance.net/funnyfun
www.delasoup.com
Portrait by Jose Morraja

**Julio Rölle @44flavours**, p072
www.44flavours.com
Portrait by Estelle Beauvais

**Maiko Gubler**, p038
maikogubler.com

**Oliver Moore
@SSAWSTUDIO**, p077
olivermoore.de
SSAWstudio.com

**ICE CREAM FOR FREE™**, p024
www.icecreamforfree.com

**Rilla Alexander**, p080
byrilla.com

**Robert Hanson**, p055
www.robertsamuelhanson.com

**Ryu Itadani**, p059
www.ryuitadani.com

**Sera Yong**, p090
www.serayong.com

**Stahl R**, p073
www.stahl-r.com

**Studio Laucke Siebein**, p023
www.studio-laucke-siebein.com

Timo Gaessner
@123buero, p047
www.123buero.com
www.milieugrotesque.com

## Industrial

Björn Andersson @Björn
Andersson Studio, p062
bjornanderssonstudio.com

Mark Braun, p054
www.markbraun.org
Portrait by Mathias Ritzmann

Tino Seubert, p037
www.tinoseubert.com

## Multimedia

Luciano Foglia, p098
www.lucianofoglia.com

Stephan Hartmann @908, p100
www.908video.de

Timm Kekeritz @Raureif, p076
www.kekeritz.com

ZWEIDREI, p033
zweidrei.eu
Portrait by Elisabeth Lanz

## Music

A Nice Idea Every Day, p019
www.aniceideaeveryday.com

Jan Paul Herzer
@hands on sound, p015
www.janpaulherzer.de

Joy Wellboy, p099
www.joywellboy.be

Kristín Björk Kristjánsdóttir,
@Kira Kira, p071
www.kirakira.is
Portrait by Goran Vejvoda

Michael Rosen, p061
www.digitalinberlin.de
www.madeiradig.com
www.mmiff.com

Siriusmo, p064
www.facebook.com/siriusmo

## Photography

Anna Rose, p074
www.annarosephoto.com

Daniel Bolliger, p026
www.danielbolligerstudio.com

Robert G. Bartholot, p101
www.bartholot.net

## Publishing

Eva Gonçalves
@Unfinished Inventory, p057
www.unfinishedinventory.com

Florian Bayer, p027
www.florianbayer.com
Portrait by Patrick Desbrosses

## Photo & other credits

**abc Art Berlin Contemporary, p028, 038–039**
(p028, 038) abc 2013 opening by Stefan Korte; (top) artwork by Michael Sailstorfer, Johann König (p039 clockwise) installation view of Solar Bell L, 2013, by Tomás Saraceno, (carbon fiber tubes, laminated solar foil, aluminium), 5 x 6.12 x 6.12m (TS 065), photo by Esther Schipper; installation view of Untitled (Monday & Tuesday), 2013, by Eva Berendes, (Stahl, Lack) at abc 2013, courtesy of Sommer & Kohl, Jacky Strenz, photo by Stefan Korte; Das gute, alte L-Thema, 2006 Maschine by Andreas Fischer, 3 x 1 x 3.2 m, courtesy of the artist and Johann König, Berlin; abc 2013 opening by Stefan Korte, artwork by Pae White & neugerriemschneider

**Bauhaus-Archiv, p016**
(Exterior) Karsten Hintz, (Chair) Fotostudio Bartsch. Courtesy of Bauhaus-Archiv Berlin

**Berliner Unterwelten, p026**
©Berliner Unterwelten e.V

**Ehemalige Jüdische Mädchenschule, p046**
(Interior) Stefan Korte

**Da Baffi, p082–083**
(p082 dish) Federico Testa (p083 bottom) ©Da Baffi

**Martin-Gropius-Bau, p034**
(p034 top) Installation view of "Tür an Tür Polen – Deutschland. 1000 Jahre Kunst und Geschichte" ©Jansch, 2011; (bottom) Martin-Gropius-Bau Restaurant & Bookshop ©Martin-Gropius-Bau, Vorbeck, 2012; atrium, Veranstaltungseinblick ©Jansch, 2011; (p035 top) Martin-Gropius-Bau exterior ©Jansch, 2013 (Right page bottom) Installation view of "Kompass. Zeichnungen aus dem Museum of Modern Art New York" ©Jansch, 2011

**Michelberger Hotel, p096**
(Facade) ©Michelberger Hotel

**Plus One Berlin, p116**
Architecture by Paola Bagna and JP Coss (CossA)

**Salon zur wilden Renate, p090**
(Pictures & bed) ©Salon zur Wilden Renate

**ST. AGNES, p042**
©St. Agnes (Exterior) Ludger Paffrath (Bottom) left: exhibition Alicja Kwade, 2013; right: exhibition Jeppe Hein, 2013; by Roman MÑrz

**Tautes Heim, p113**
(All) Ben Buschfeld

–
In Accommodation: all courtesy of respective hotels

# CITIX60

## CITIx60: Berlin

Published and distributed by
viction workshop ltd

## viction:ary™

7C Seabright Plaza, 9-23 Shell Street,
North Point, Hong Kong

Url: www.victionary.com
Email: we@victionary.com
- www.facebook.com/victionworkshop
- www.twitter.com/victionary_
- www.weibo.com/victionary

Edited and produced by viction:ary

Concept & art direction: Victor Cheung
Research & editorial: Queenie Ho, Caroline Kong
Project coordination: Katherine Wong, Jovan Lip
Design & content map illustration: Cherie Yip

Editing: Elle Kwan
Cover map illustration: Vesa Sammalisto
Count to 10 illustrations: Guillaume Kashima aka Funny Fun
Photography: Vivi Abelson

© 2014, 2015 viction workshop ltd

All rights reserved. No part of this publication may be reproduced, stored in retrieval systems or transmitted in any form or by any means, electronic, mechanical, photocopying, recording or any information storage, without written permissions of viction:ary.

Content is compiled based on facts available as of February 2014. Travellers are advised to check for updates from respective locations before your visit.

Third edition
ISBN 978-988-12227-5-6
Printed and bound in China

### Acknowledgements

A special thank you to all creatives, photographer(s), editor, producers, companies and organisations for your crucial contributions to our inspiration and knowledge necessary for the creation of this book. And, to the many whose names are not credited but have participated in the completion of the book, we thank you for your input and continuous support all along.

# CITIX60
City Guides

**CITIx60** is a handpicked list of hot spots that illustrates the spirit of the world's most exhilarating design hubs. From what you see to where you stay, this city guide series leads you to experience the best — the places that only passionate insiders know and go.

Each volume is a unique collaboration with local creatives from selected cities. Known for their accomplishments in fields as varied as advertising, architecture and graphics, fashion, industry and food, music and publishing, these locals are at the cutting edge of what's on and when. Whether it's a one-day stopover or a longer trip, **CITIx60** is your inspirational guide.

Stay tuned for new editions.

Featured cities:

**Amsterdam**
**Barcelona**
**Berlin**
**Hong kong**
**London**
**Los Angeles**
**New York**
**Paris**
**Tokyo**